THIS BOOK

IS FOR:

____

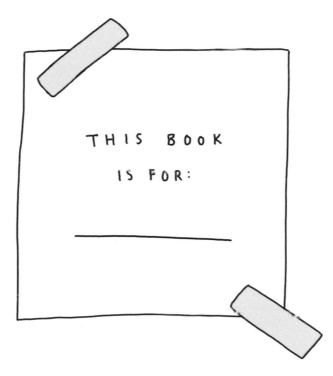

ALL OF THIS IS FOR YOU

A LITTLE BOOK OF KINDNESS

BY RUBY JONES

HarperOne
An Imprint of HarperCollins*Publishers*

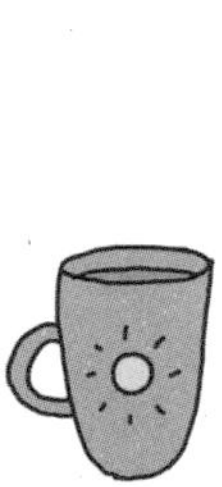

A LITTLE NOTE

This book originally came about as the result of an illustration I did on 15 March 2019 with the words "this is your home and you should have been safe here." The illustration was my immediate response to the terror attacks at two mosques in Christchurch, New Zealand. I had shared it online the afternoon of the attacks and was humbled to see the image take on a life of its own in the most beautiful and overwhelming way.

In early 2020, a year on from that event, the entire world has found itself being impacted by the devastating outbreak of Covid-19. Each confined to our homes, grieving together—at worst, for lives lost to this; at best, grieving for lives we're afraid we may not have again, for jobs we are unsure of or know we have lost, for people we love who can't share our safe place, for the warm embraces we crave but can't have because social distancing, face masks and gloves are in the way.

Living through this time is something most of us would have never dreamt of and there is nothing easy about it. But it can be done, and must be done with love and compassion—for ourselves and for others, for the places we call home, for this beautiful earth. The seismic effects of living through this time will bring profound changes to our communities in ways we don't yet know, but holding on to the small kindnesses that make us human and keep us connected are more important than ever.

I hope throughout these times you can find some small comfort in this book, that on any given day, rain or shine, happy tears or painful ones, you can open it and find a page that speaks to you. My work explores human connection and emotion, the ways in which we can be kinder to ourselves, to the people in our lives and to the world around us. I try to give a voice to those tender moments in life that we sometimes hold close and murmur about only to ourselves: our dreams, fears, hopes, loves, losses. Moments experienced by people of all ages and genders, and members of all religions, ethnicities and cultures. They are what it means to be human. It's as simple as that.

Ruby Jones

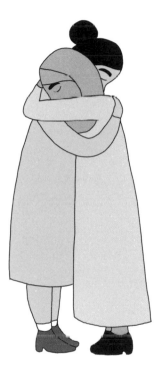

THIS IS YOUR HOME
AND YOU SHOULD HAVE
BEEN SAFE HERE

THIS CAN
ALL FEEL
SO OVERWHELMING
SOMETIMES.

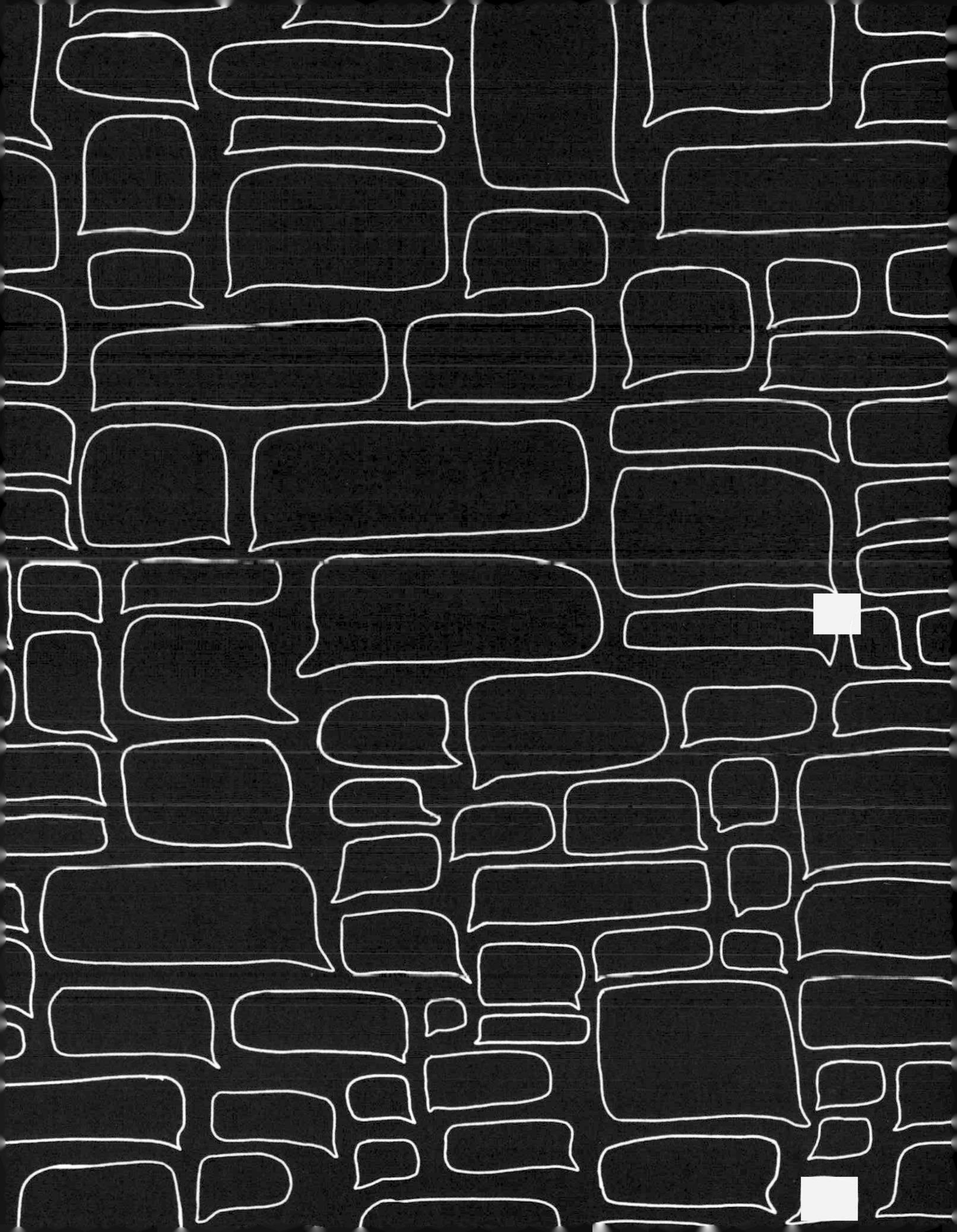

IT WON'T BE
LIKE THIS
FOREVER.

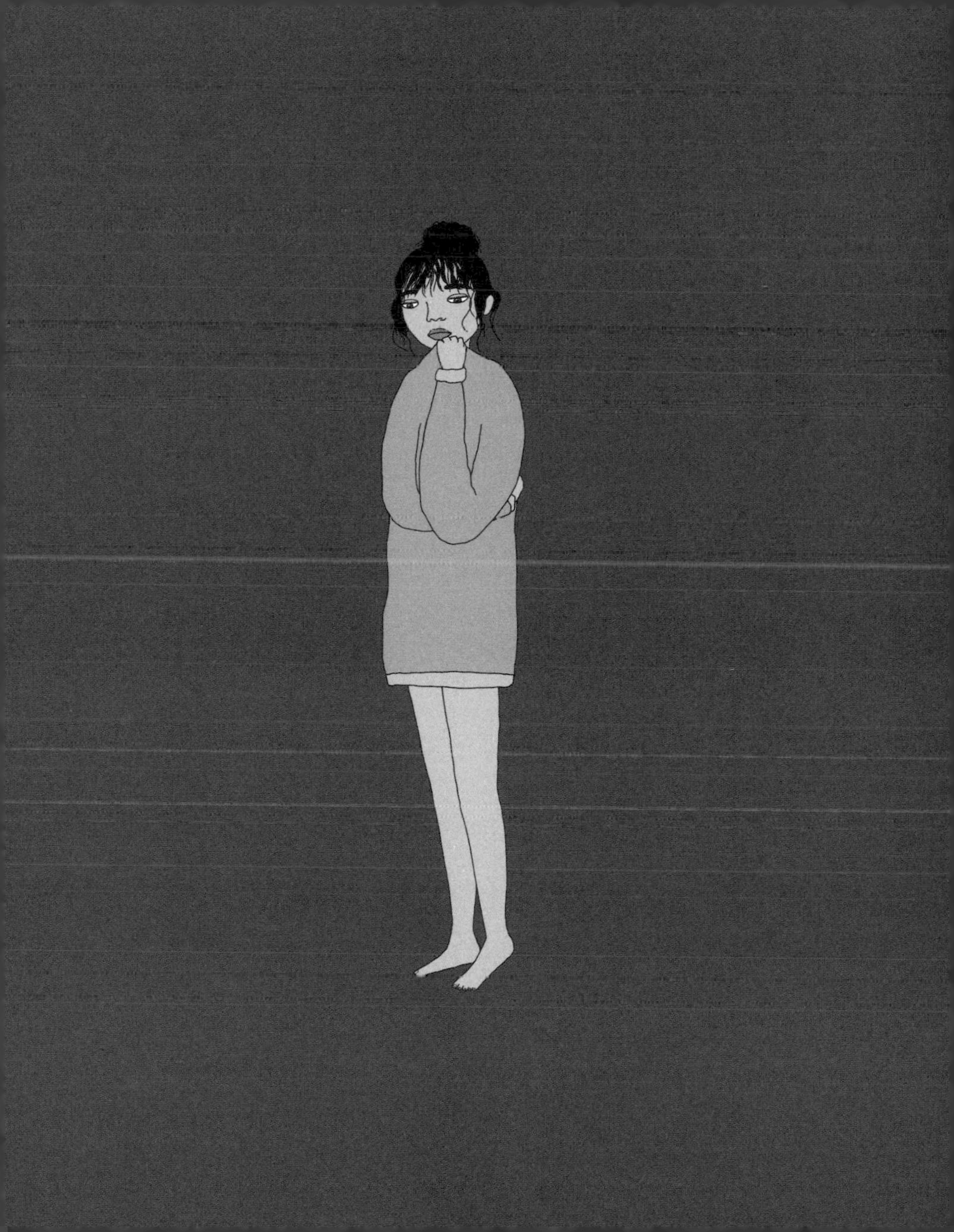

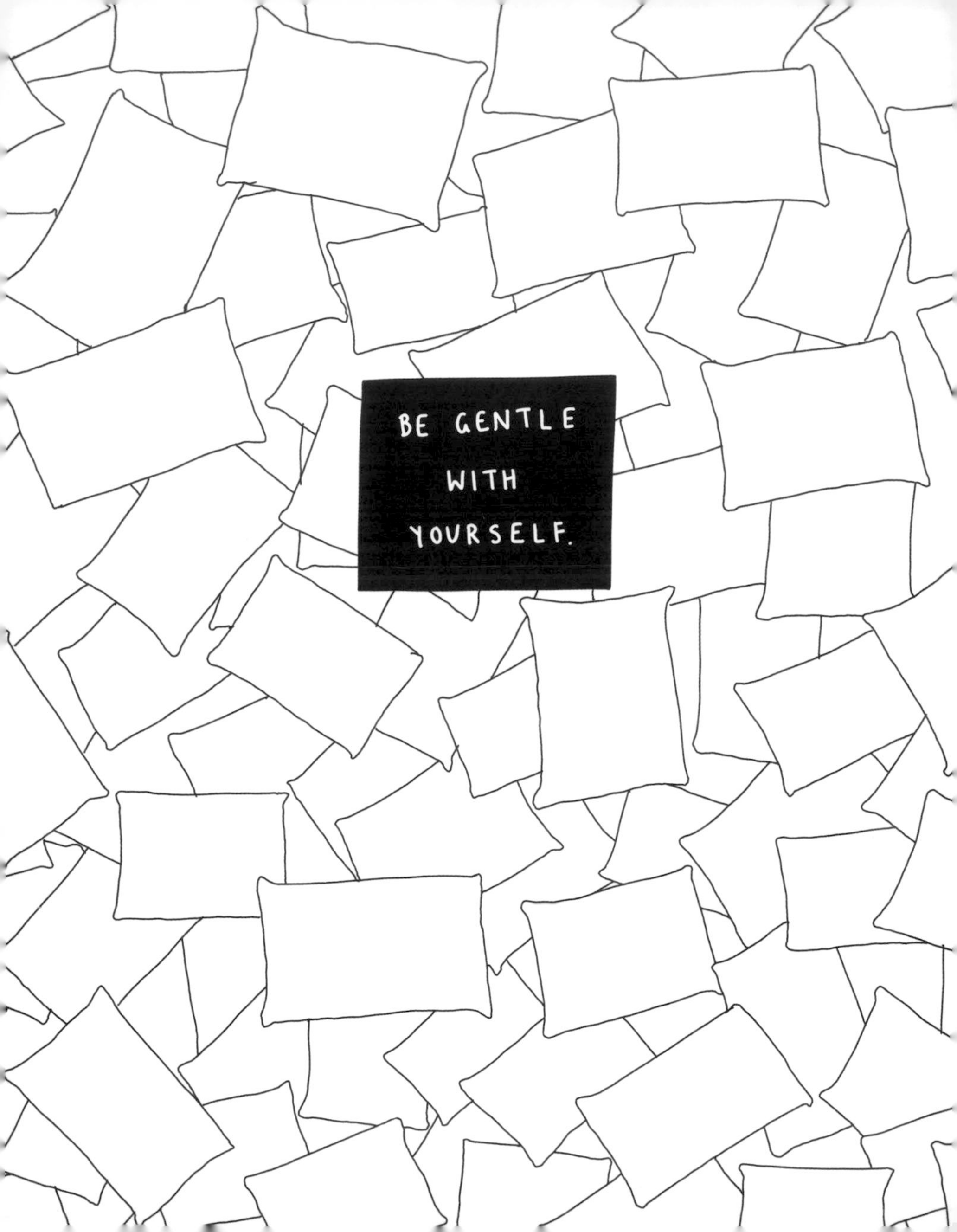
BE GENTLE
WITH
YOURSELF.

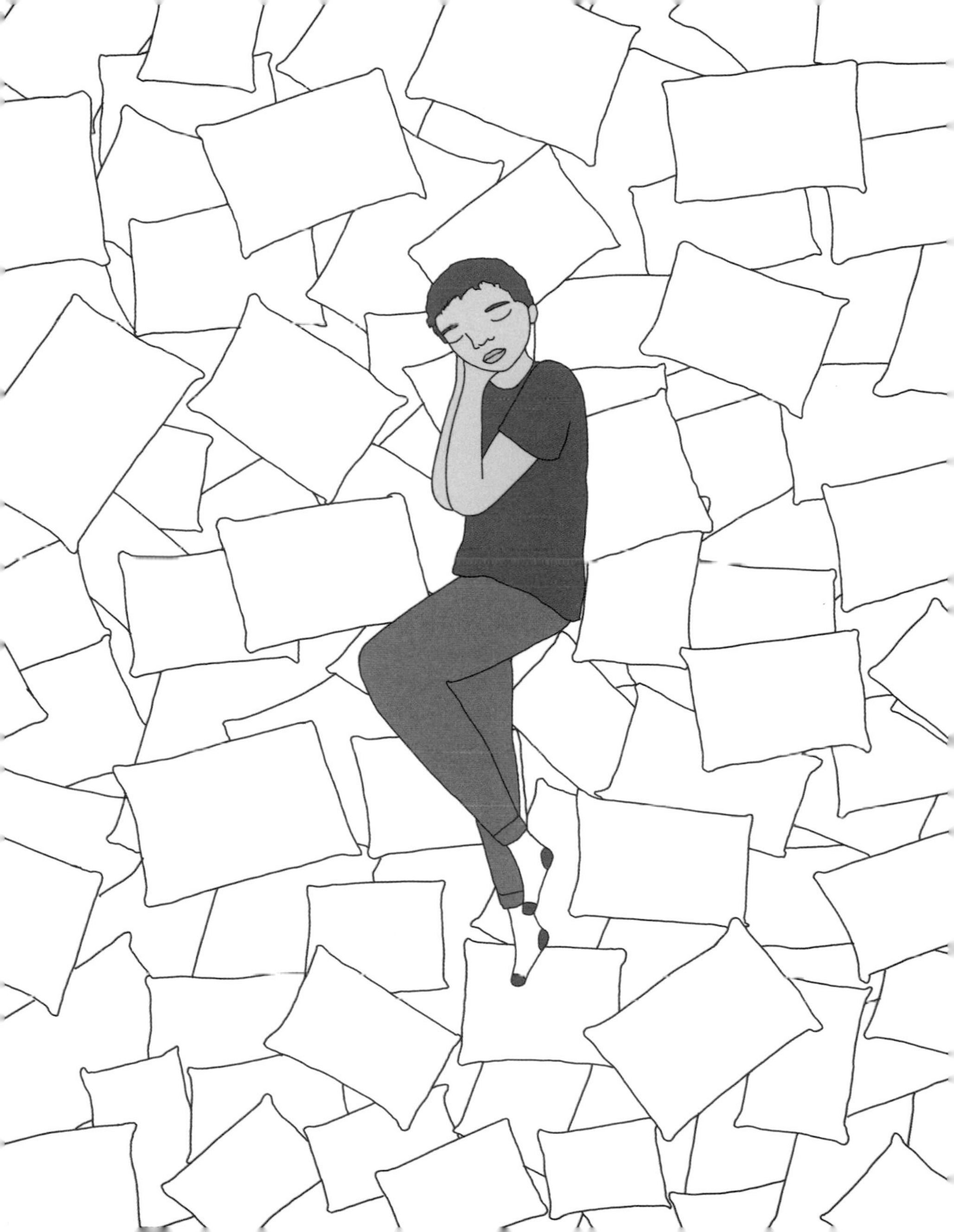

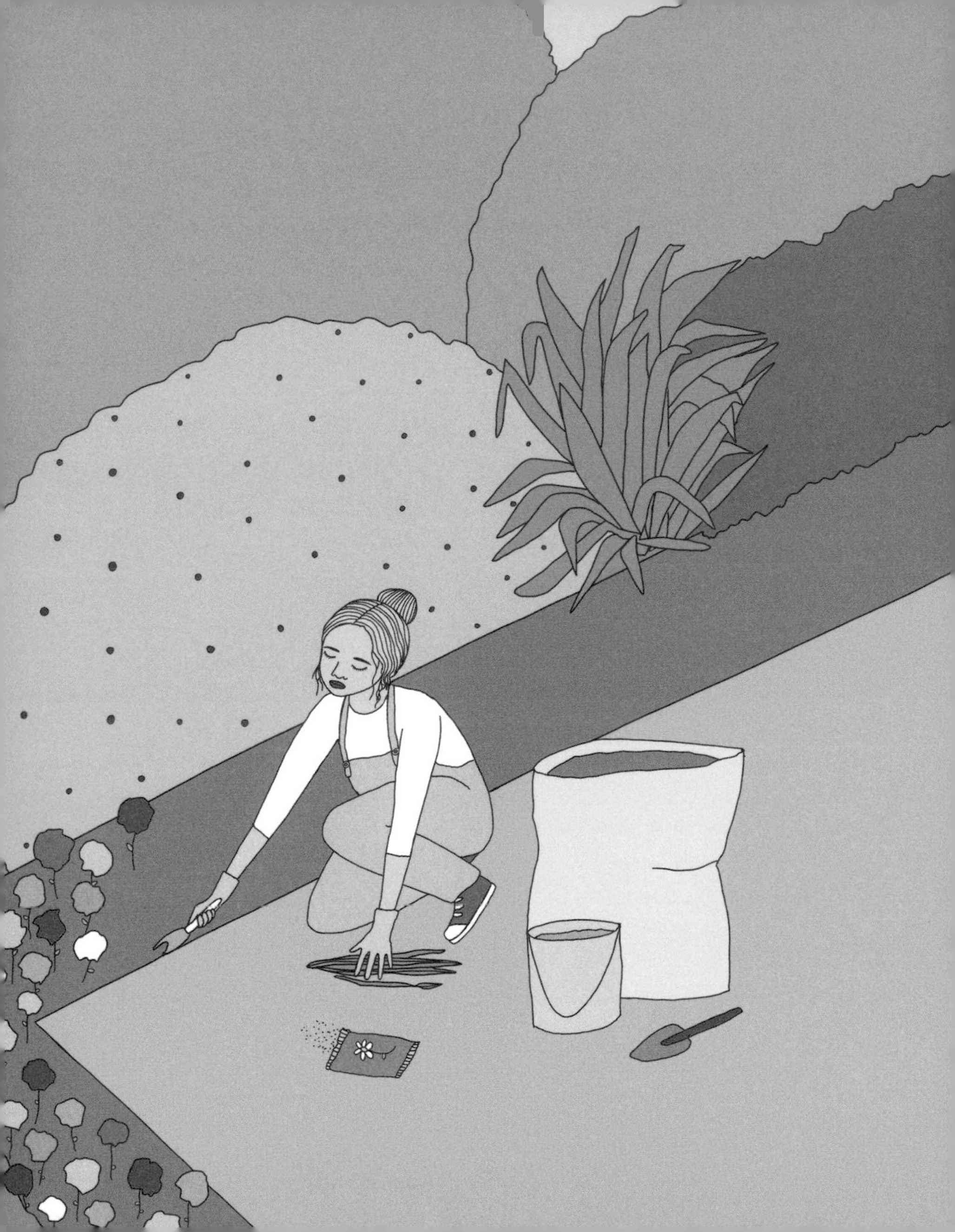

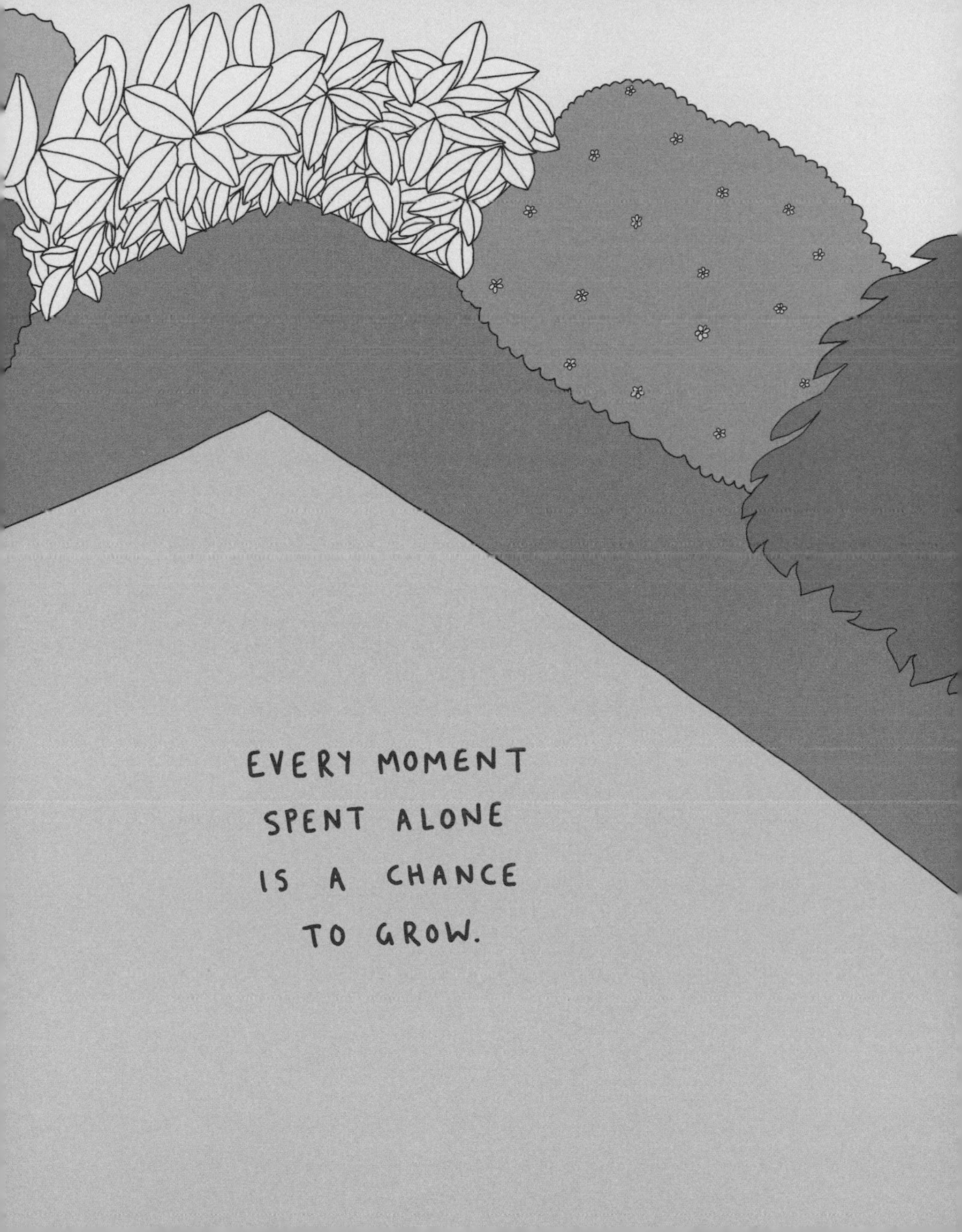

EVERY MOMENT
SPENT ALONE
IS A CHANCE
TO GROW.

STAY UP LATE.
WAKE UP EARLY.
PICK FLOWERS.
WATCH THE SKY.
SWIM.
DANCE.
READ.
EAT FRESH FRUIT.
SLOW DOWN.

FIND WAYS
TO BE
TOGETHER...

...NO MATTER
THE DISTANCE
BETWEEN YOU.

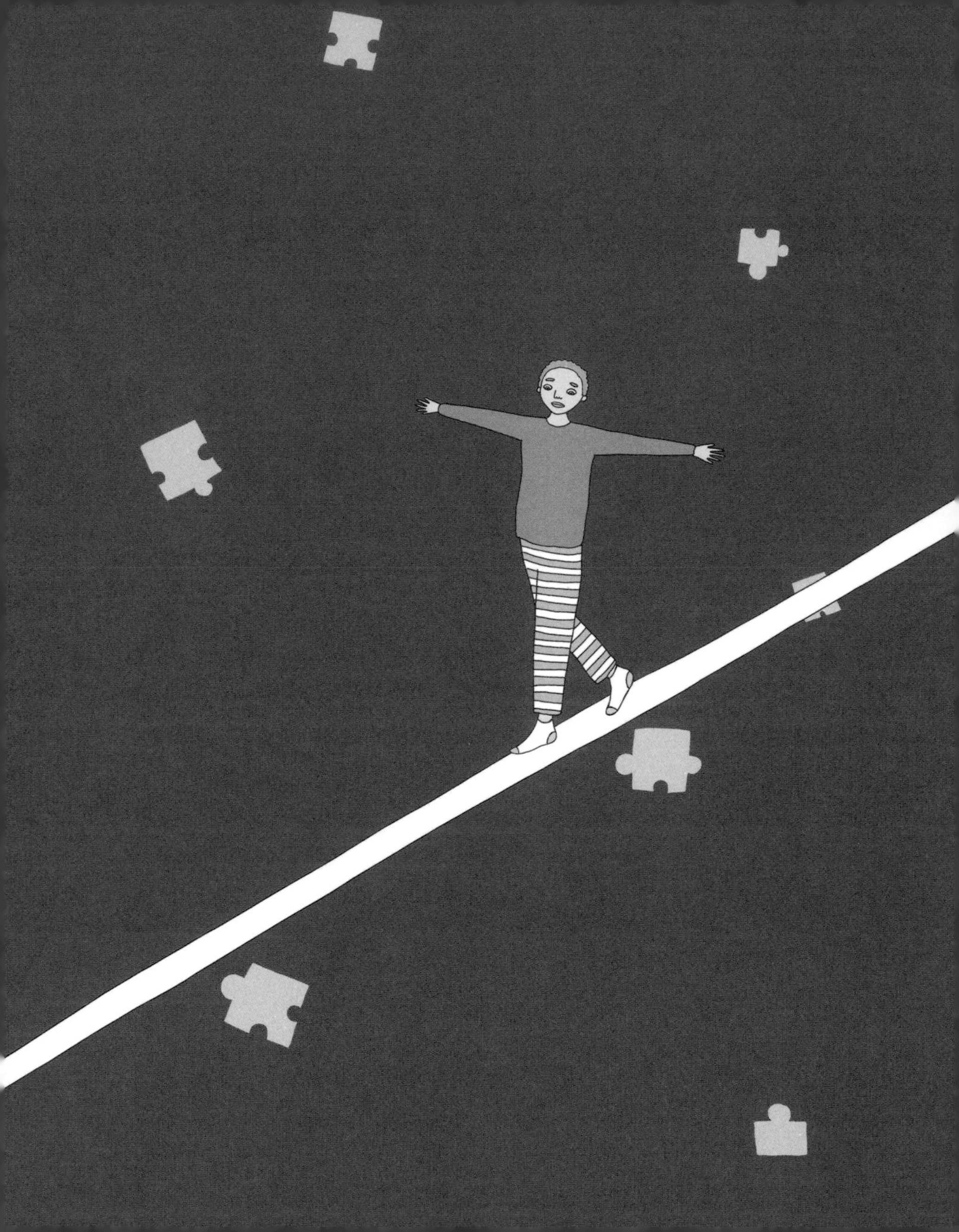

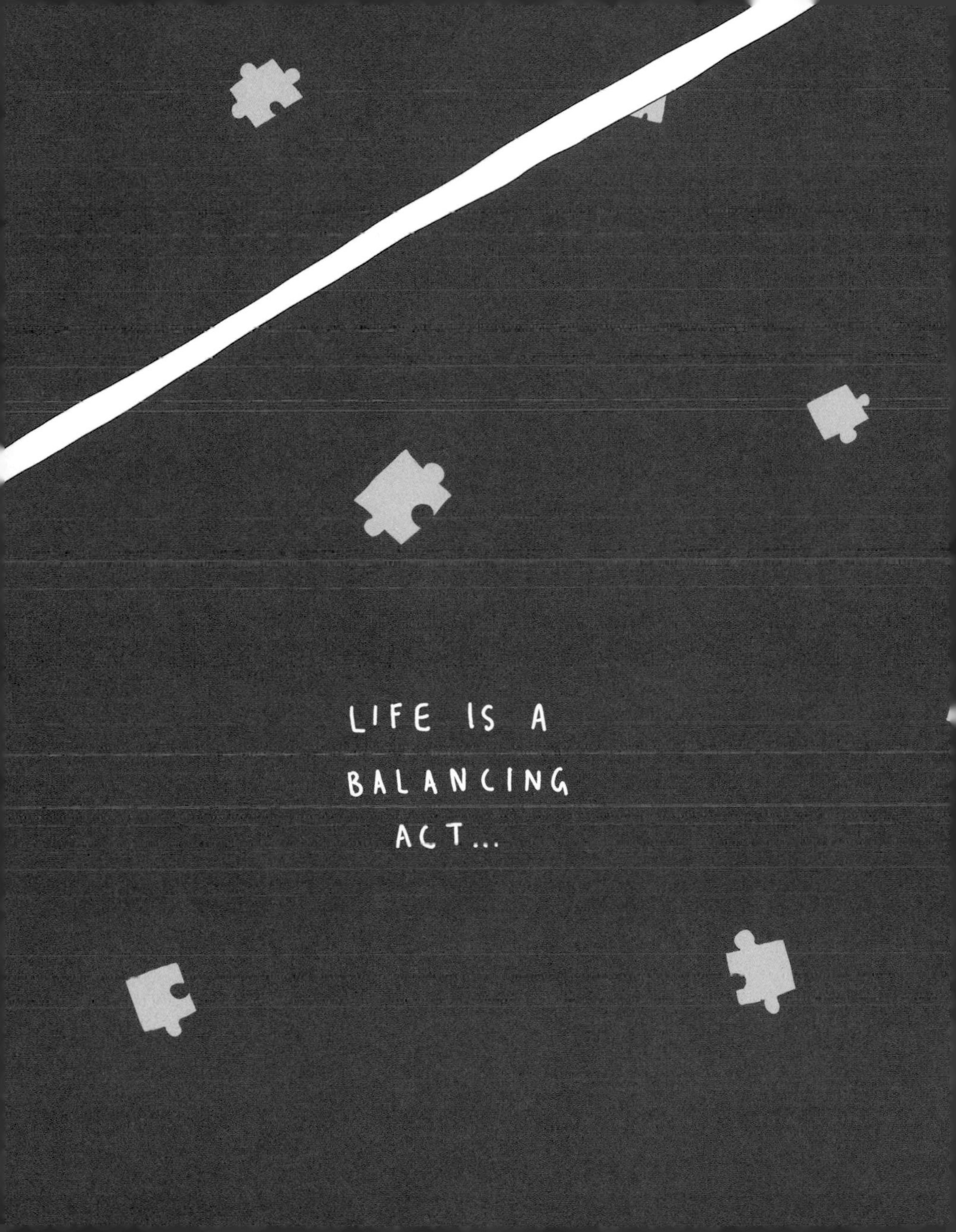
LIFE IS A
BALANCING
ACT...

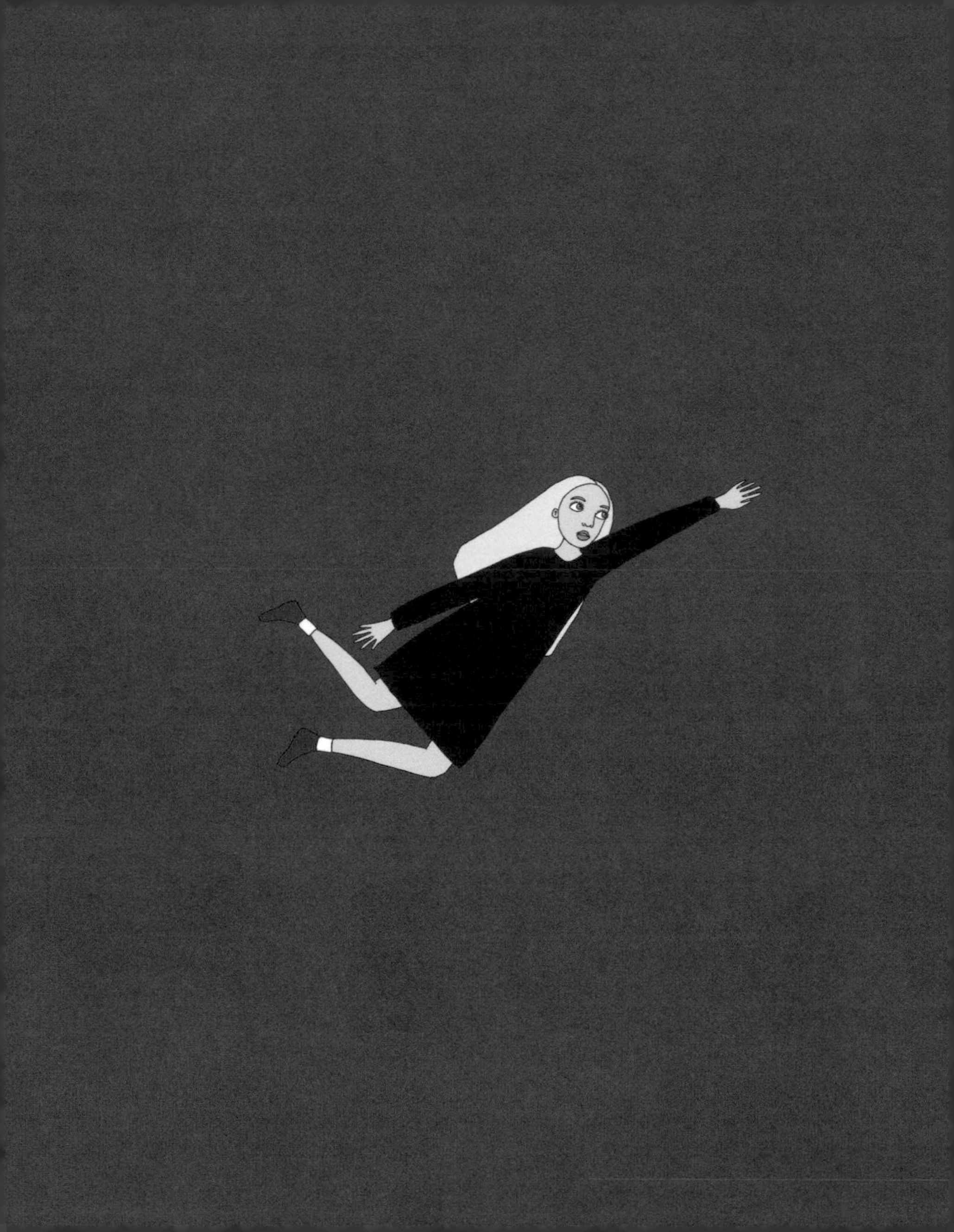

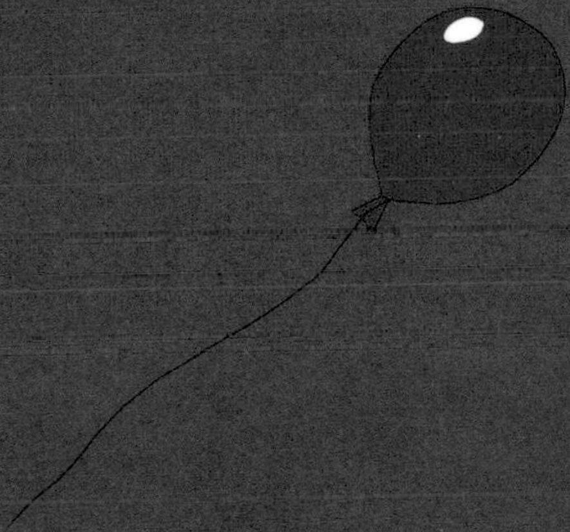

...YOU WON'T ALWAYS
GET IT RIGHT AND THAT
IS OKAY. YOU WILL FALL.
YOU WILL GET LOST.
THINGS WILL BREAK.
PEOPLE WILL LEAVE.
THAT'S ALL PART
OF THE JOURNEY.

NONE

OF

IT

IS YOUR

FAULT.

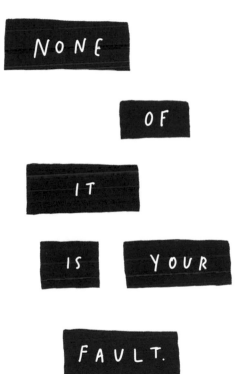

NO ONE
ELSE KNOWS
WHAT THEY'RE
DOING EITHER.

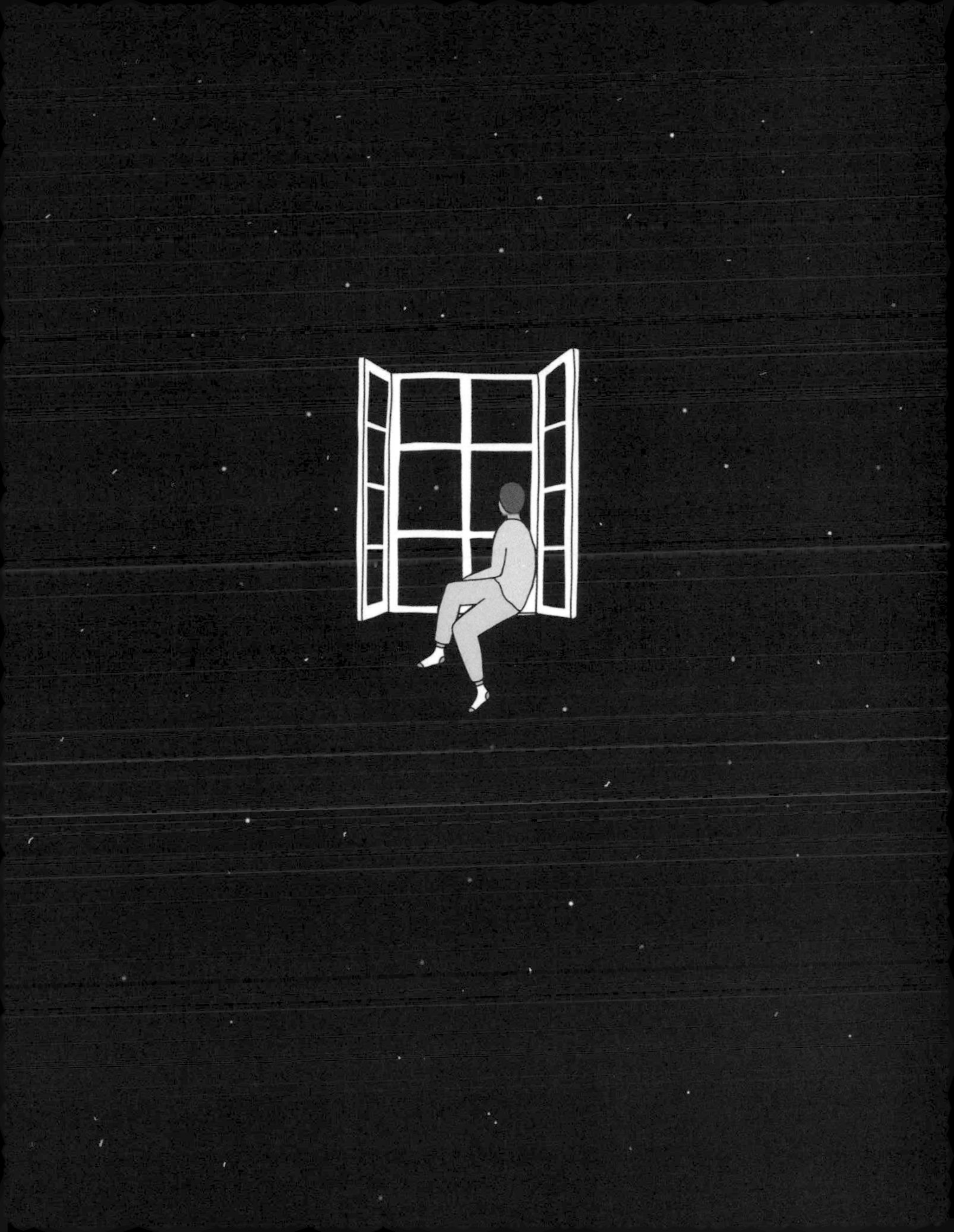

SHOWING YOUR
EMOTIONS
DOESN'T MAKE
YOU CRAZY.

YOU ARE
NOT YOUR
NEGATIVE
THOUGHTS.

STOP. CLOSE YOUR EYES.
BREATHE. NOTHING IS
GOING TO BE PERFECT
(THERE'S NO SUCH THING)
BUT EVERYTHING WILL
BE OKAY.

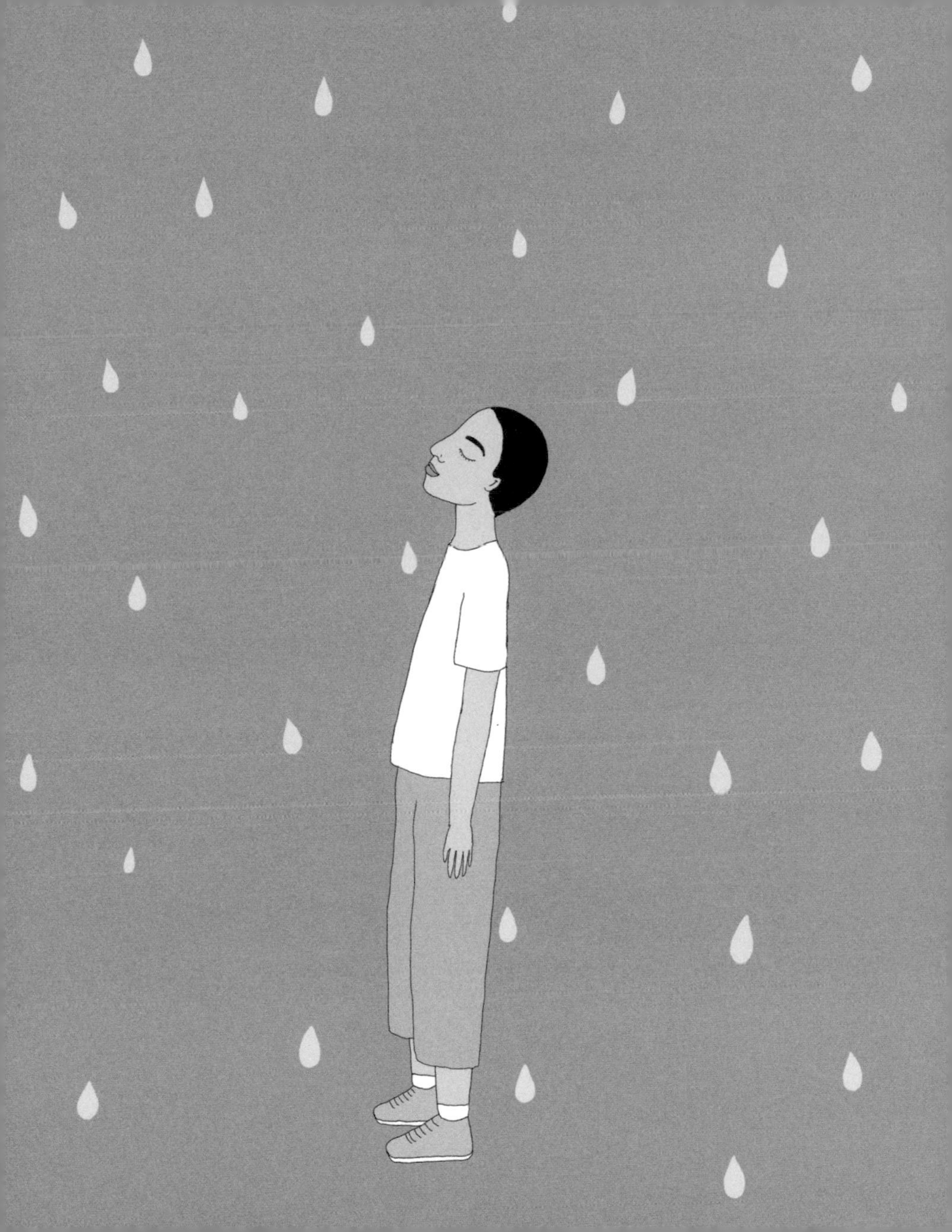

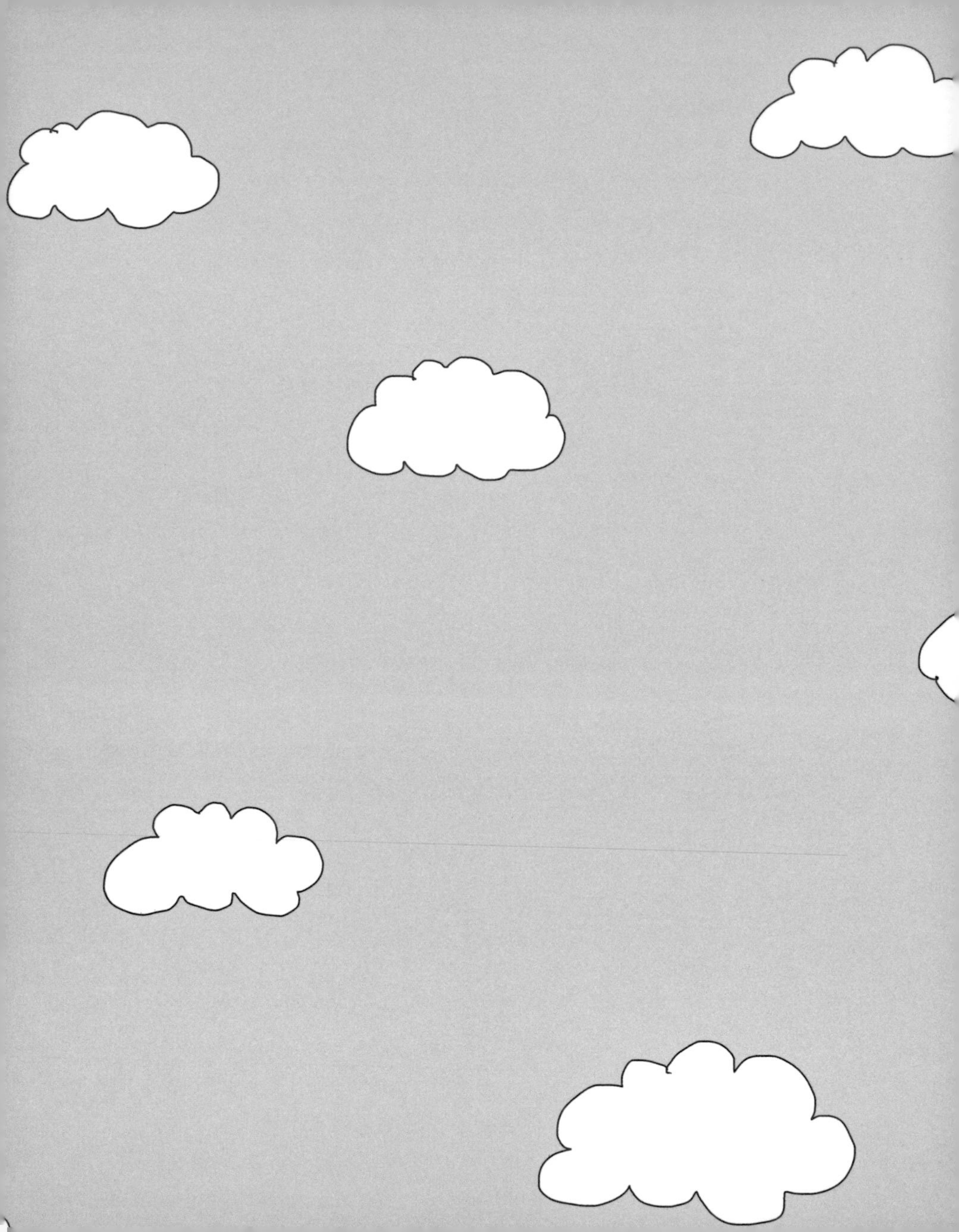

WE ARE SO
LUCKY TO
BE HERE.

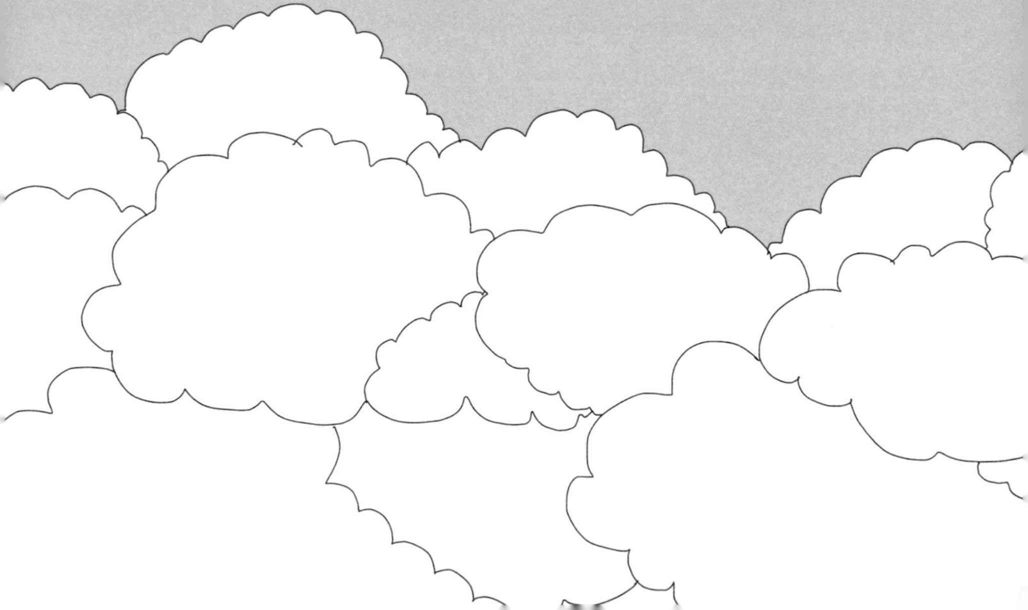

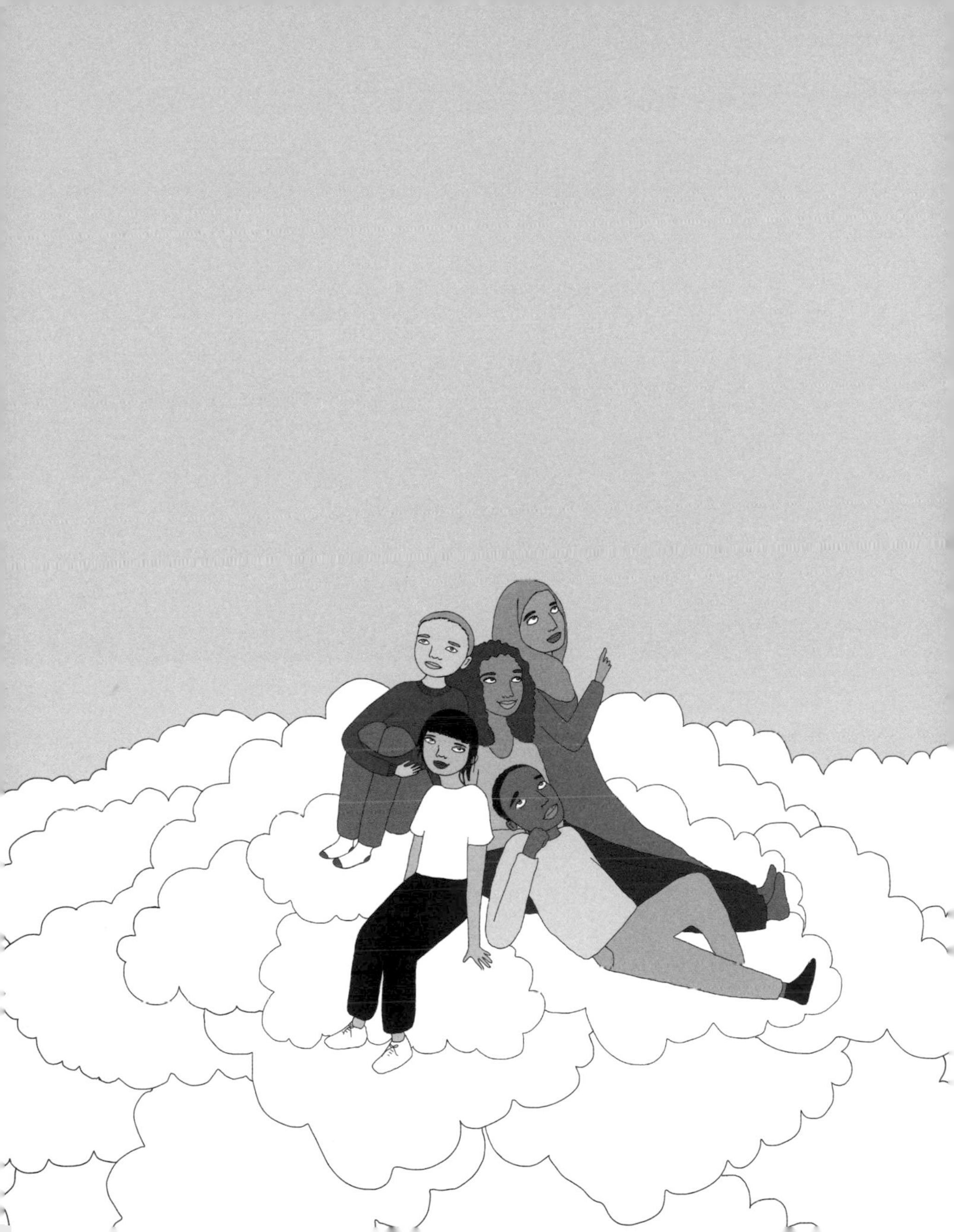

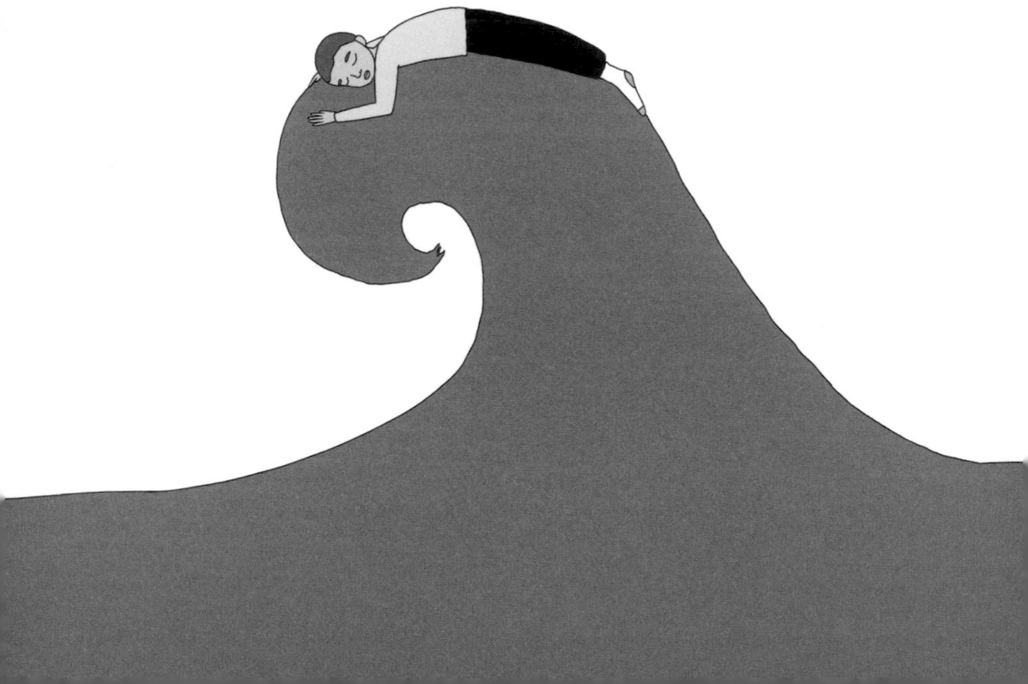

NOTHING CAN PREPARE US
FOR PEOPLE LEAVING EARLY.
GRIEF WILL COME IN WAVES.
BUT THE WAVES WILL
SUBSIDE AND THE SUN
WILL STILL RISE.

NONE OF THIS
IS EASY.
TAKE AS MUCH TIME
AS YOU NEED.

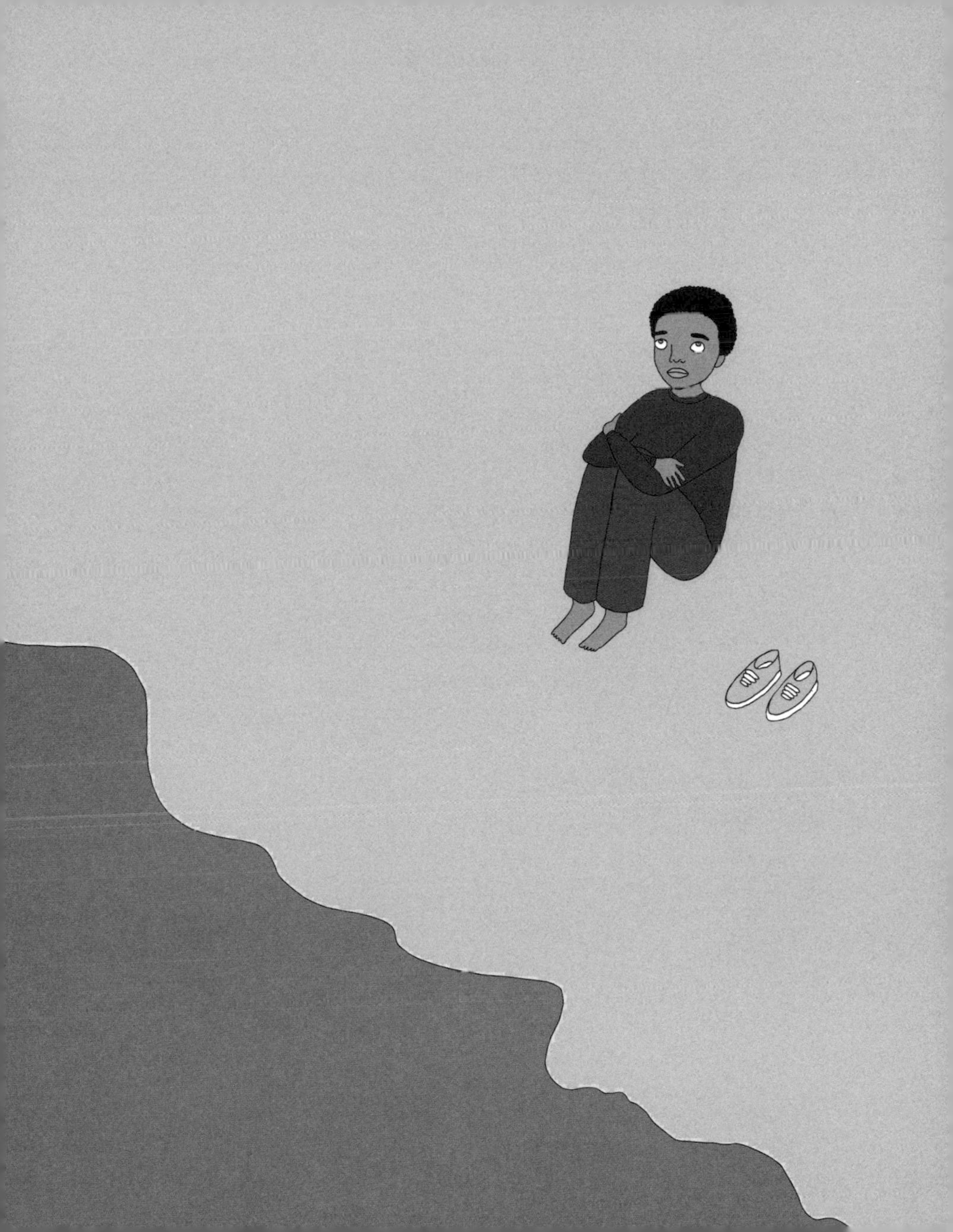

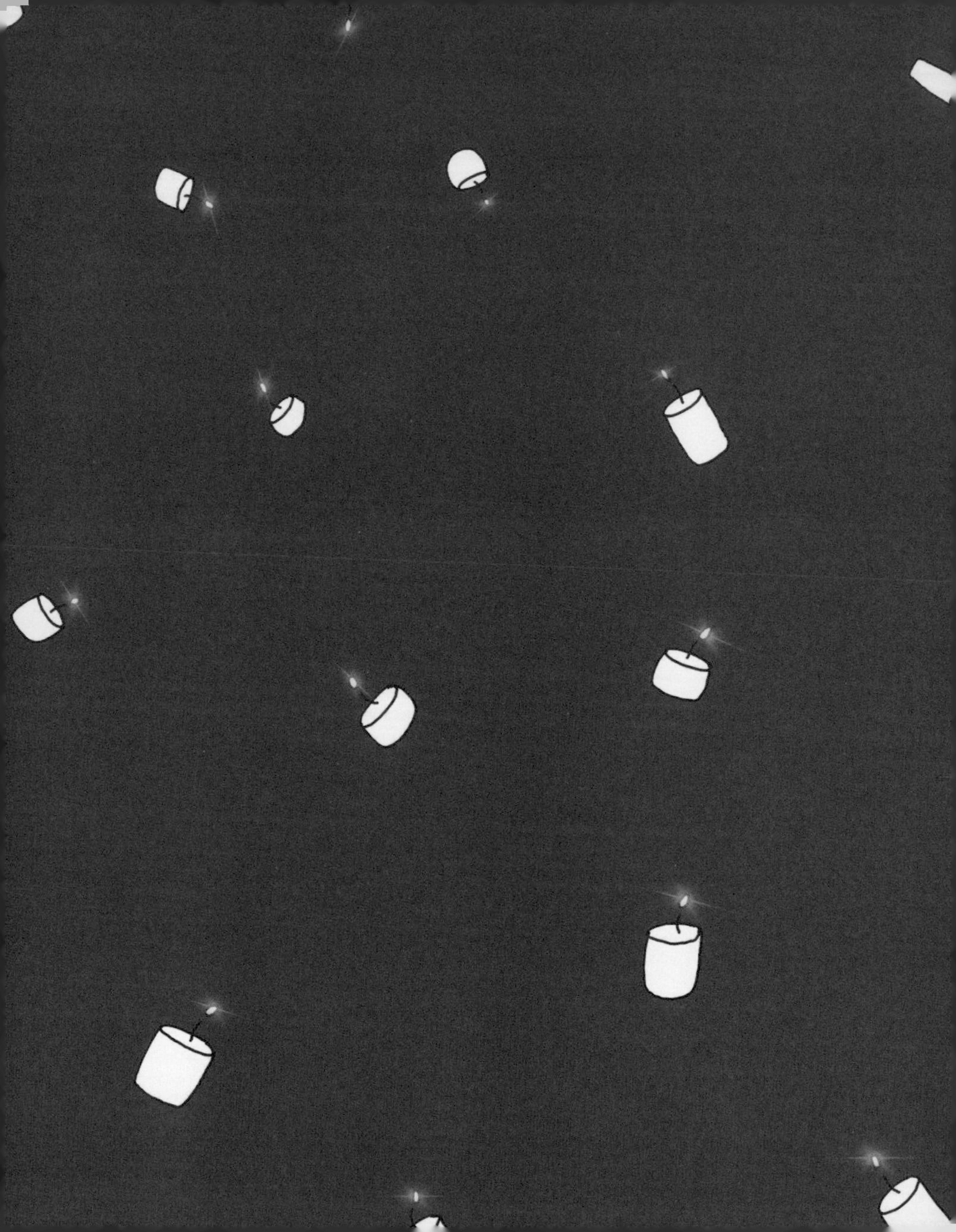

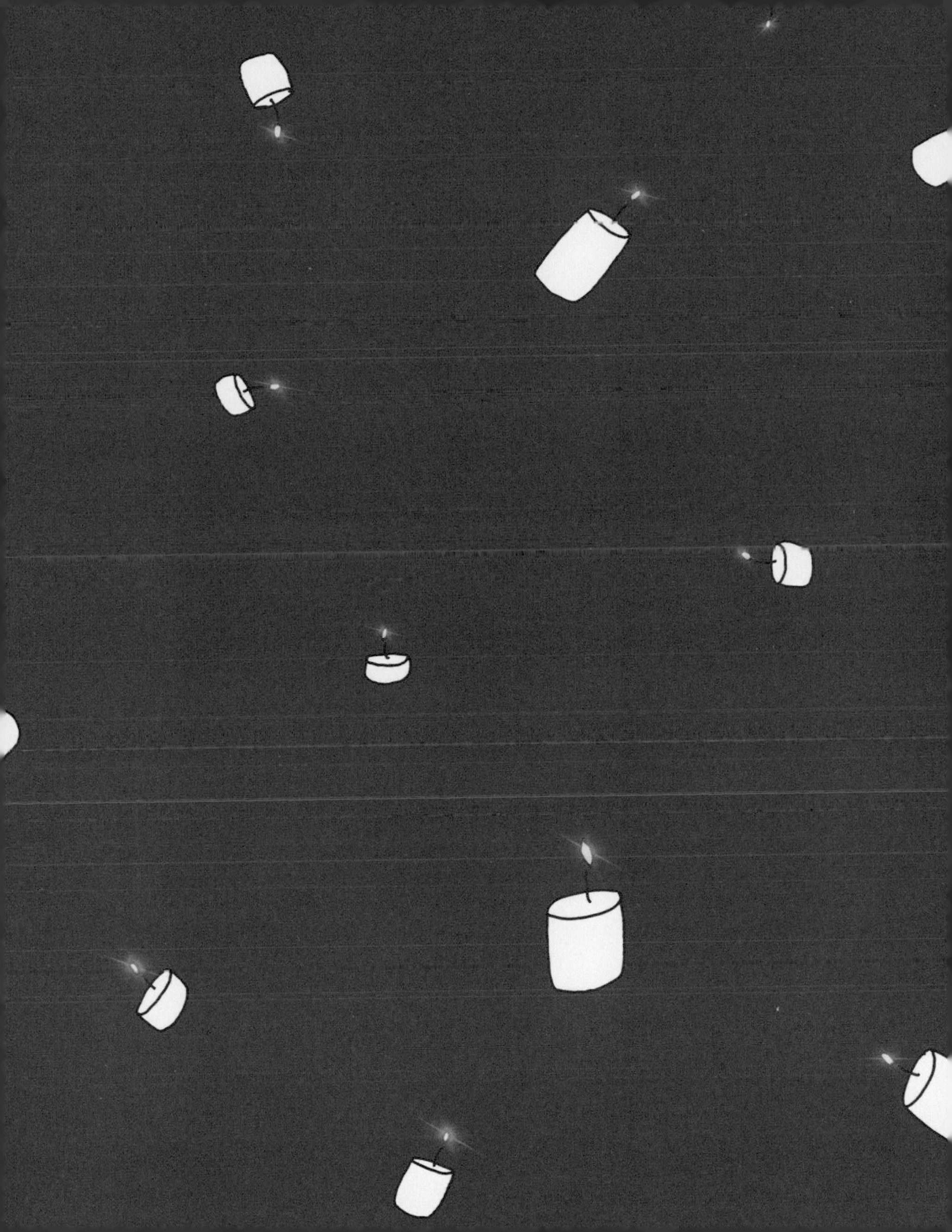

PLEASE DON'T LEAVE.
THE WORLD NEEDS
GOOD PEOPLE LIKE
YOU IN IT.

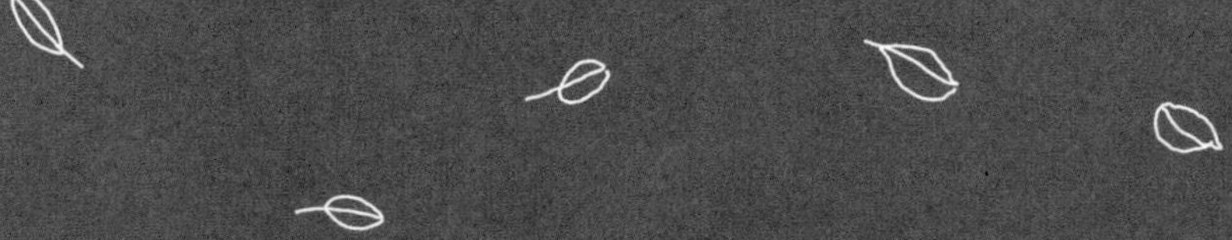

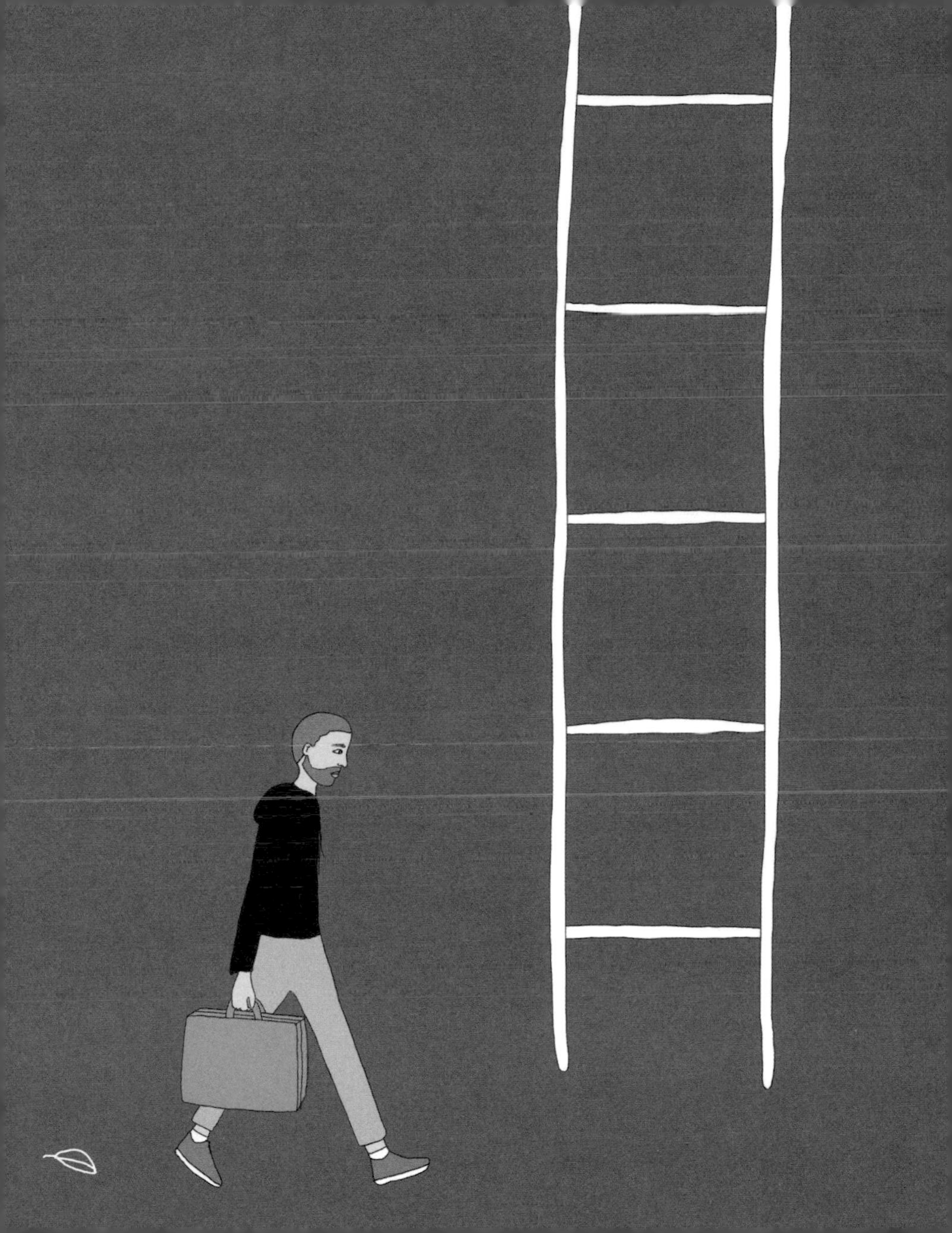

YOU ARE LOVED
SO MUCH MORE THAN
YOU COULD EVER
IMAGINE.

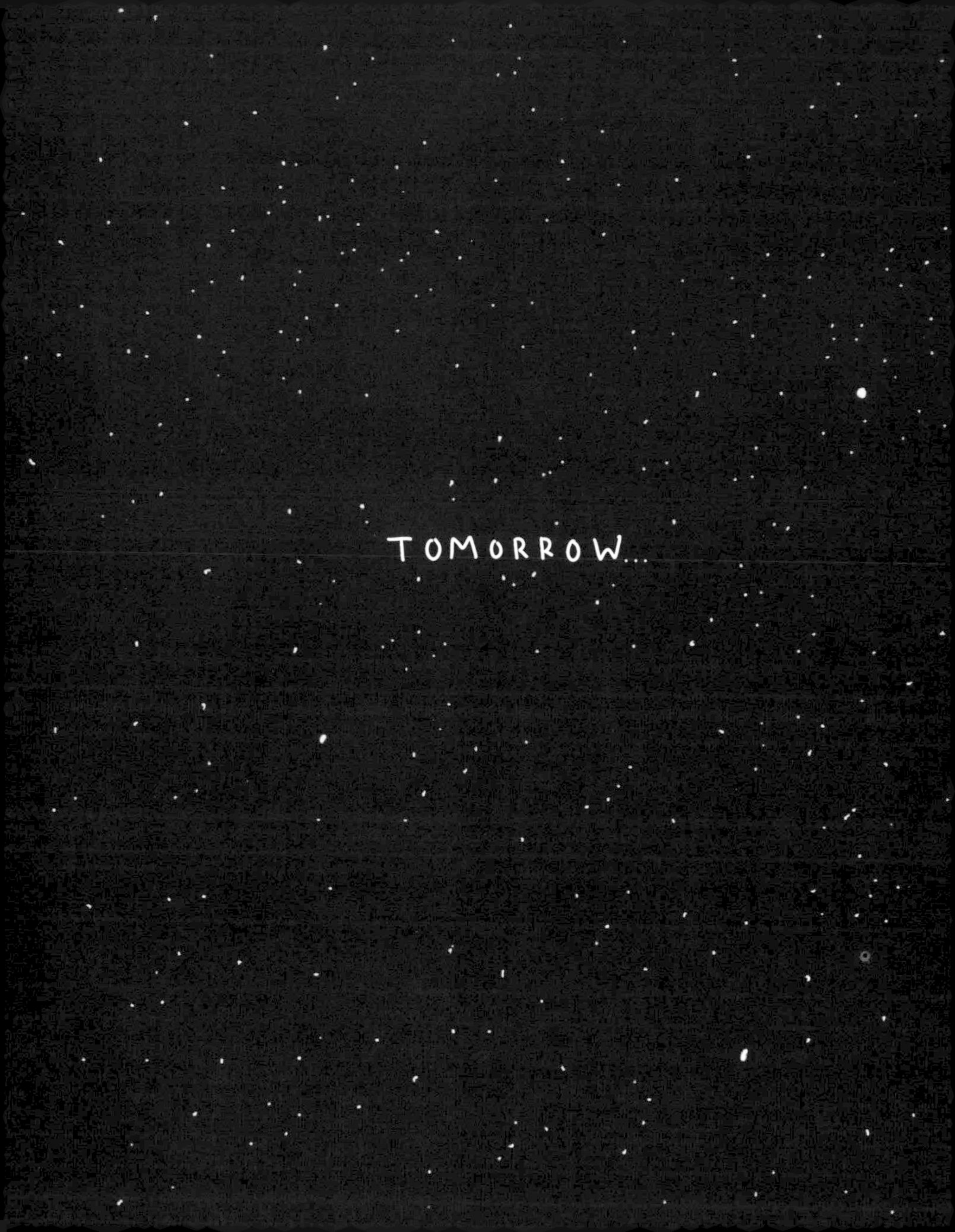
TOMORROW...

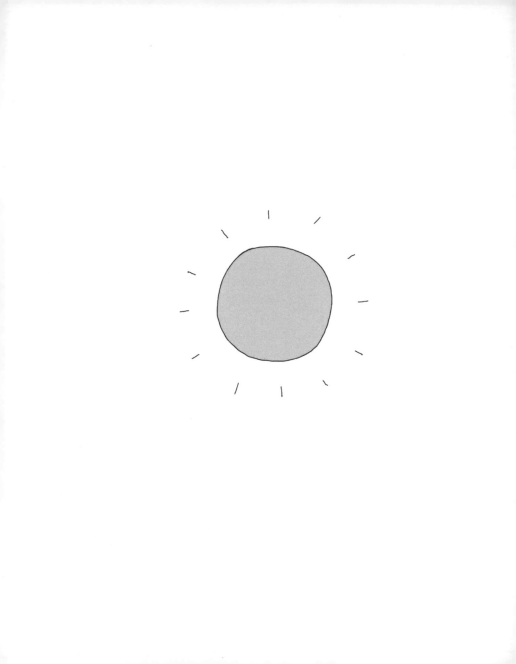

...IS A
NEW DAY.

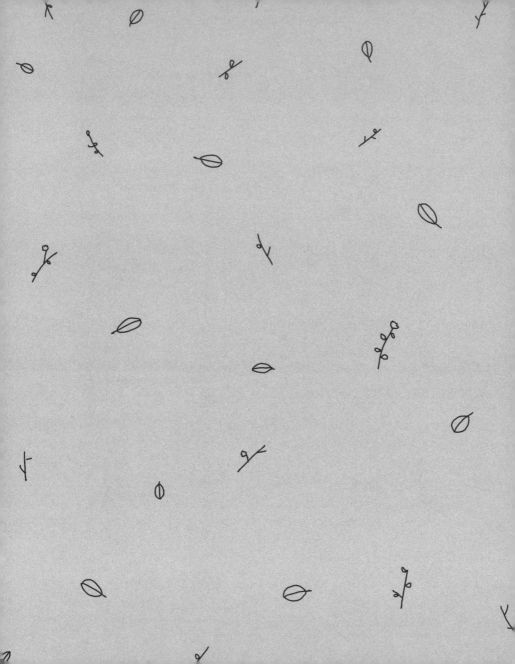

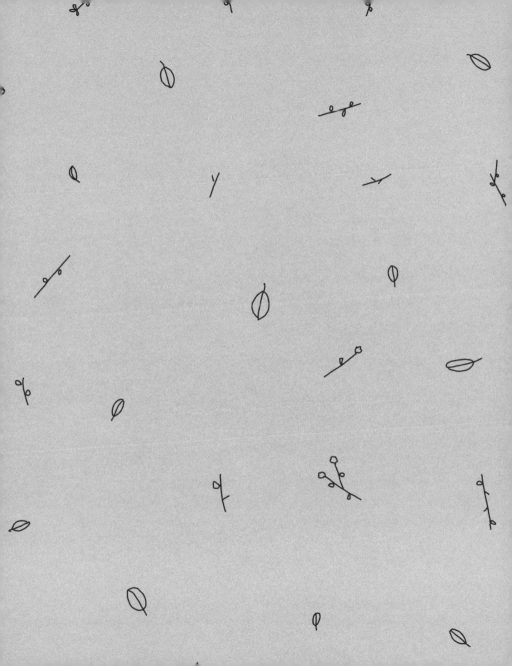

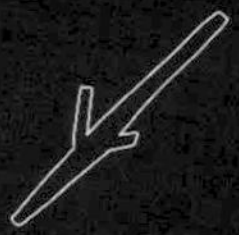

ON DAYS YOU CAN'T STAND TO
LOOK AT YOUR OWN REFLECTION,
REMEMBER ALL OF THE THINGS
YOUR BODY HAS ALLOWED YOU
TO DO AND ALL OF THE PLACES
IT HAS TAKEN YOU. IT MAY BE
SCARRED, IT MAY BE TIRED,
IT MAY BE OLD...

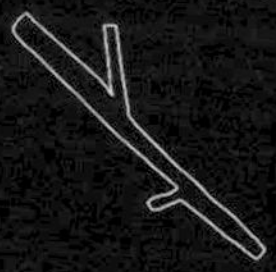

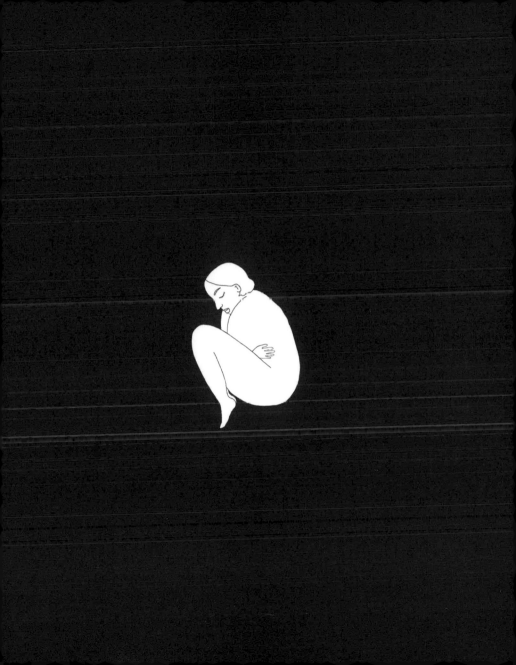

...BUT YOU ARE
SO LUCKY TO
BE IN IT.

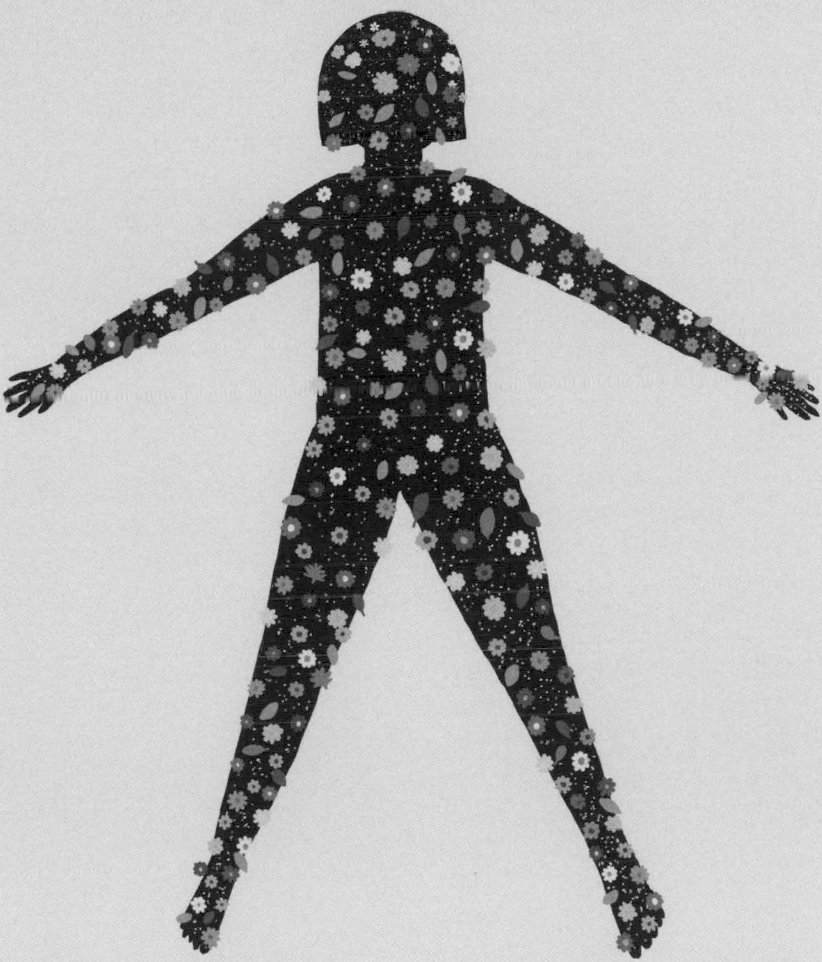

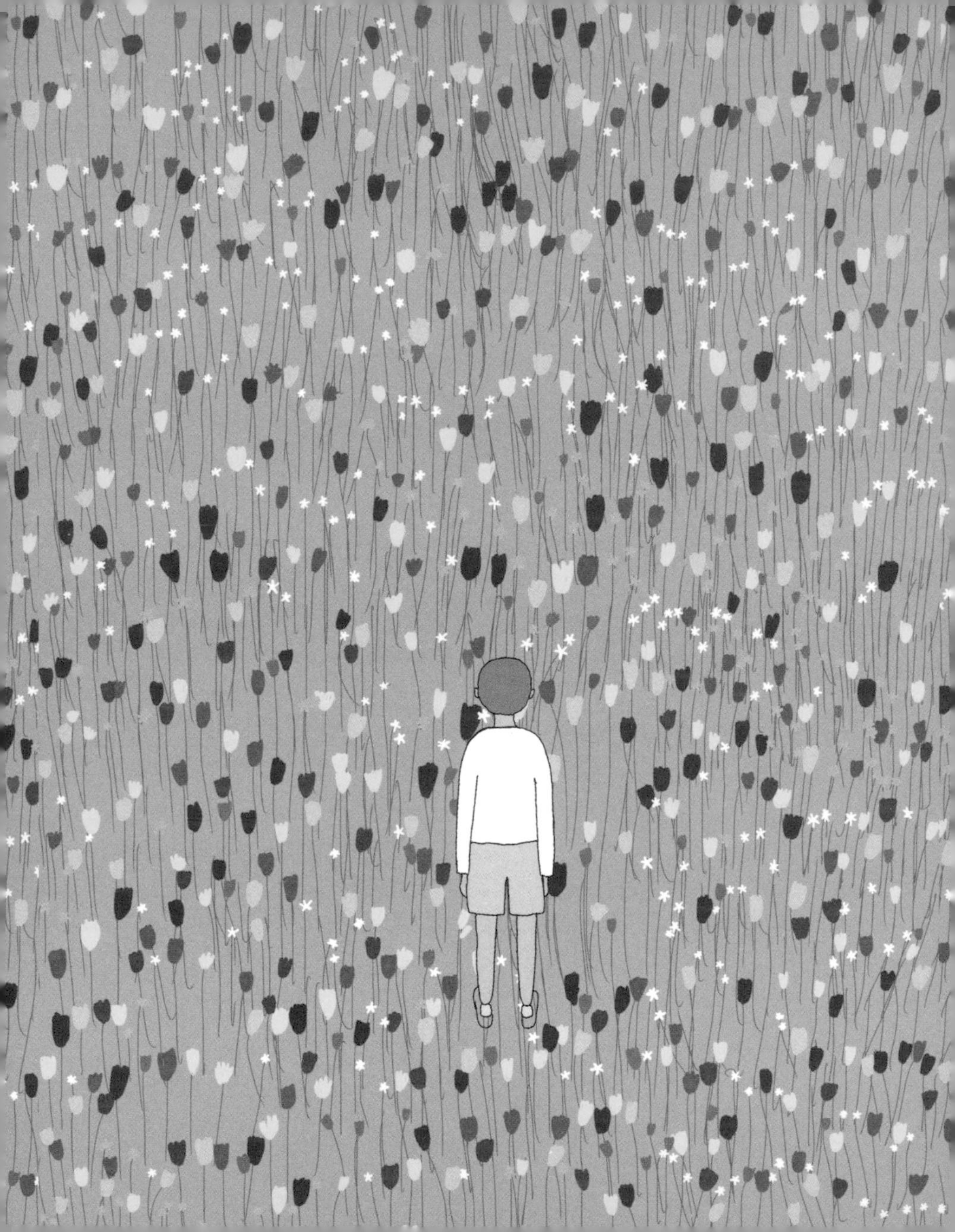

EVERY FLOWER
IS FOR YOU. EVERY RAY
OF SUNSHINE IS FOR YOU.
EVERY BIRD'S SONG
IS FOR YOU. ALL OF
THIS IS FOR YOU.

HOLD

ON.

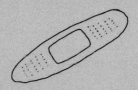

PROTECT
YOURSELF AND
EVERYTHING
YOU LOVE.

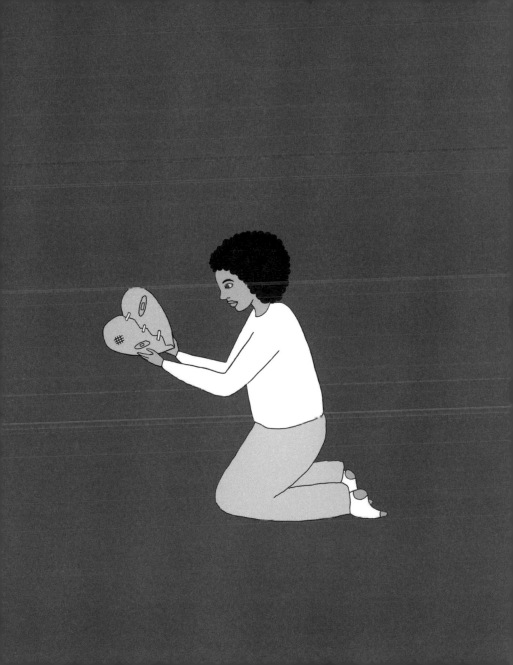

YOU ARE PRECIOUS.
YOU ARE WORTHY.
YOU ARE WHOLE.
YOU ARE ENOUGH.

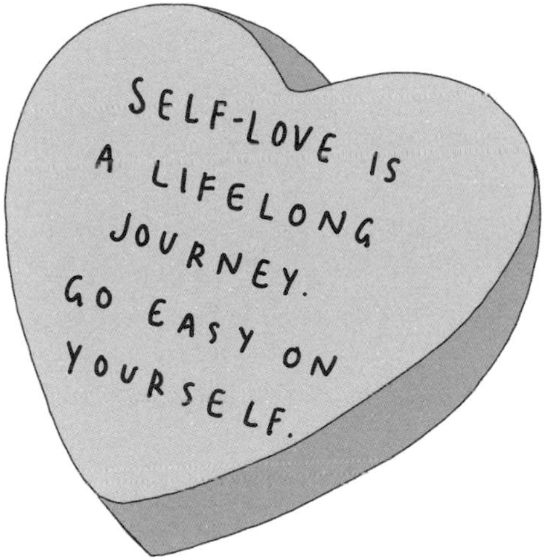
SELF-LOVE IS
A LIFELONG
JOURNEY.
GO EASY ON
YOURSELF.

LOOK AFTER YOURSELF
THE WAY YOU'D LOOK
AFTER YOUR
FIVE-YEAR-OLD SELF.

YOUR EXISTENCE IS
SOMEONE'S SUNSHINE
EVERY SINGLE DAY.

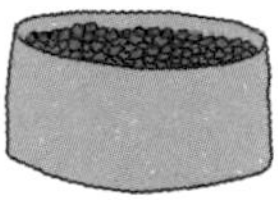

I HOPE YOU LEARN
TO SEE BEYOND THE
GAZE OF OTHERS AND
RECOGNISE HOW PRECIOUS
YOU ARE, HOW STRONG
YOU ARE AND HOW INCREDIBLY
LUCKY WE ARE TO
HAVE YOU HERE.

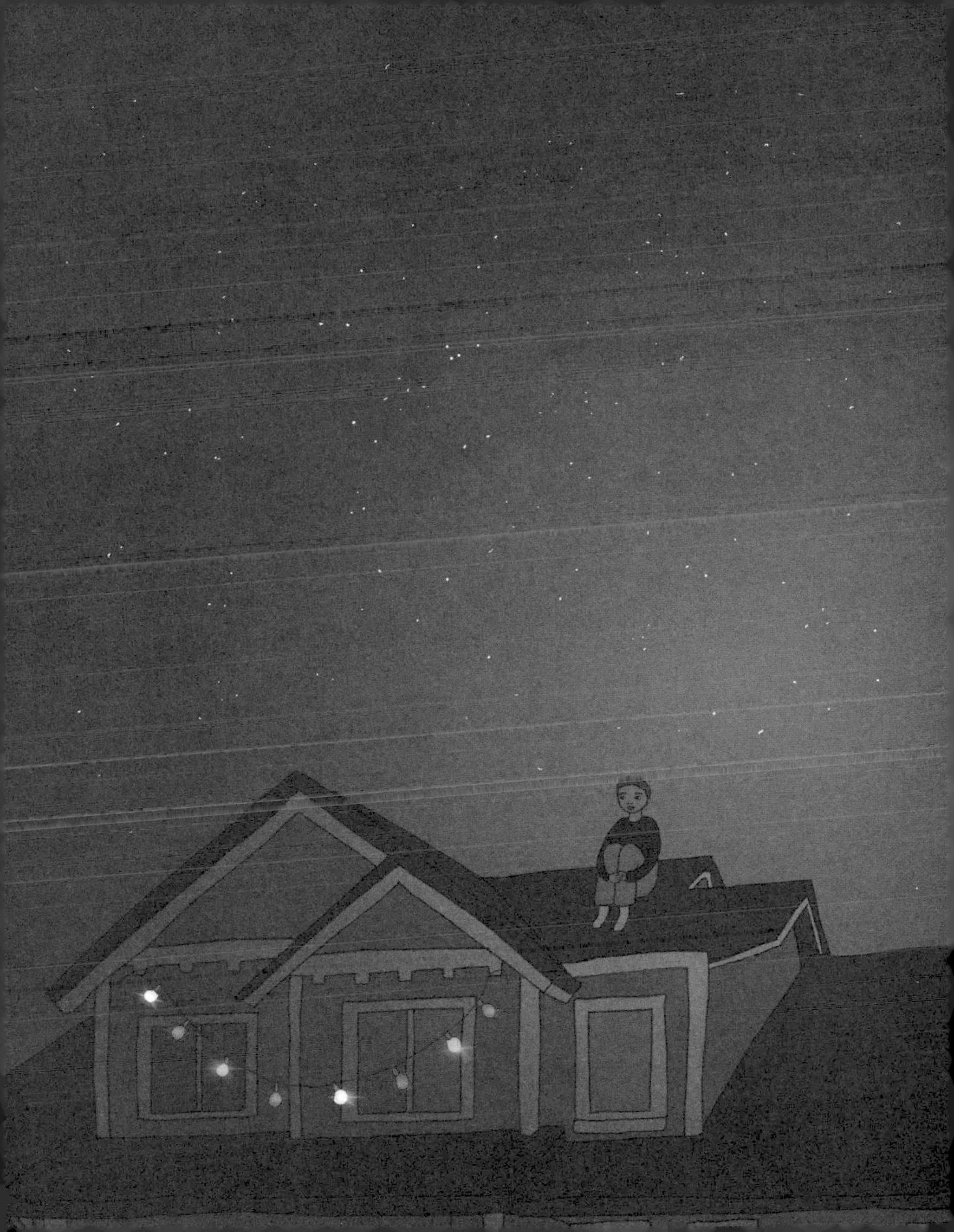

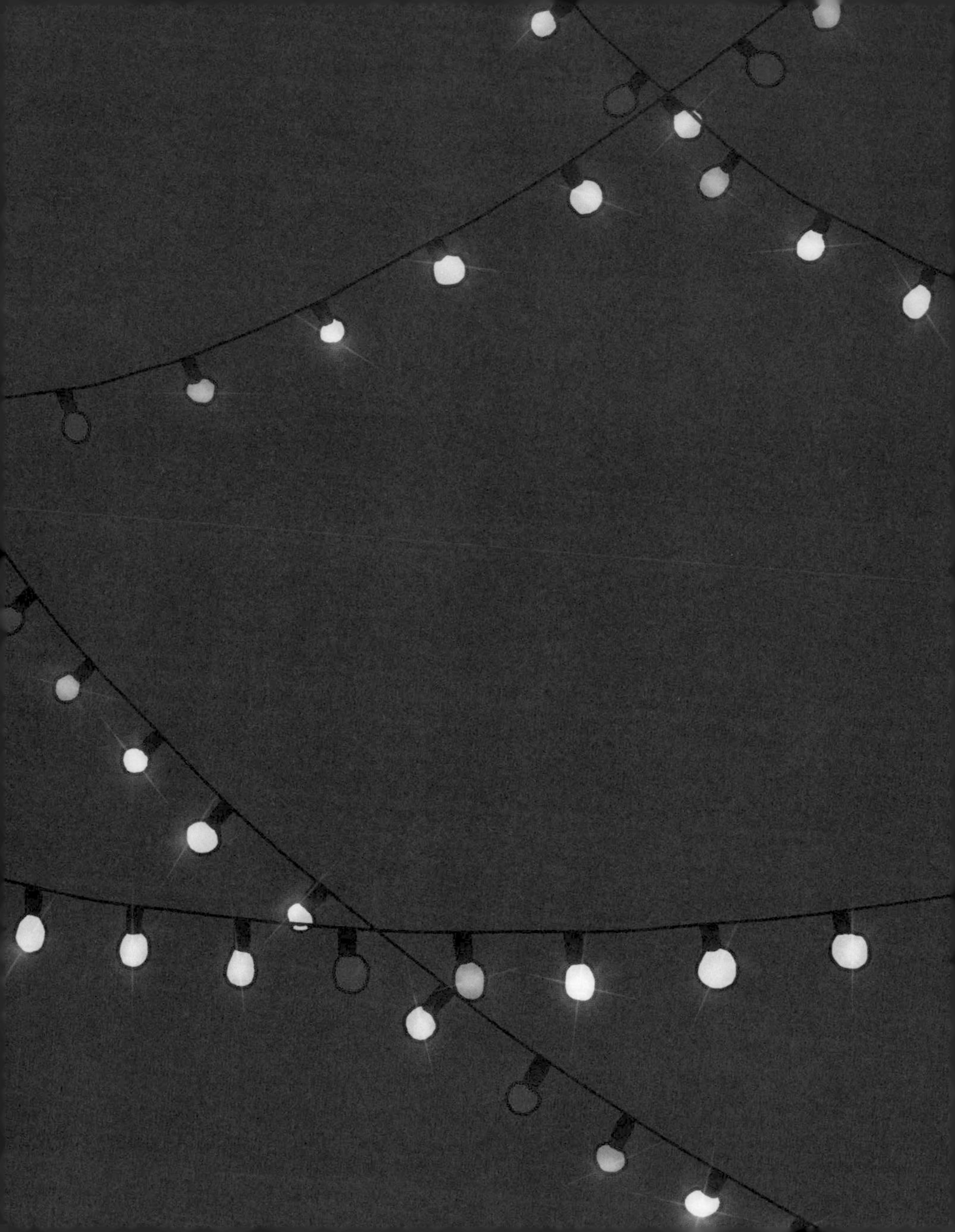

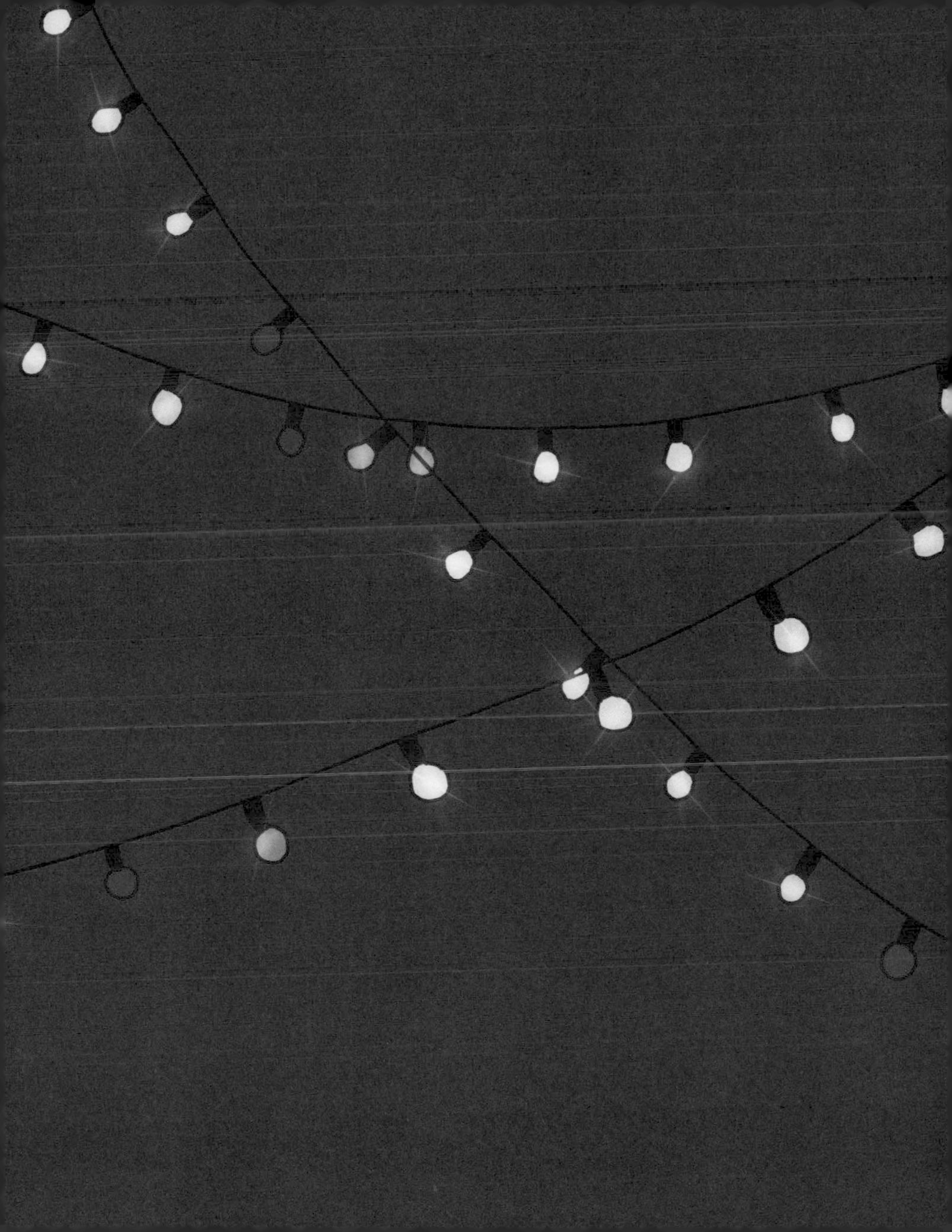

THINGS THAT DO NOT
DEFINE YOUR WORTH:

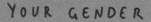
YOUR GENDER

YOUR AGE

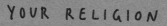
YOUR RELIGION

YOUR BANK
BALANCE

YOUR CULTURE

YOUR JOB

YOUR BACKGROUND

YOUR LAST NAME

YOUR PHYSICAL
APPEARANCE

STAND UP FOR WHAT
YOU KNOW IS RIGHT.

BE SOFT.
BE OPEN.
BE TENDER.
BE LOVING.
BE FORGIVING.
BE BRAVE.

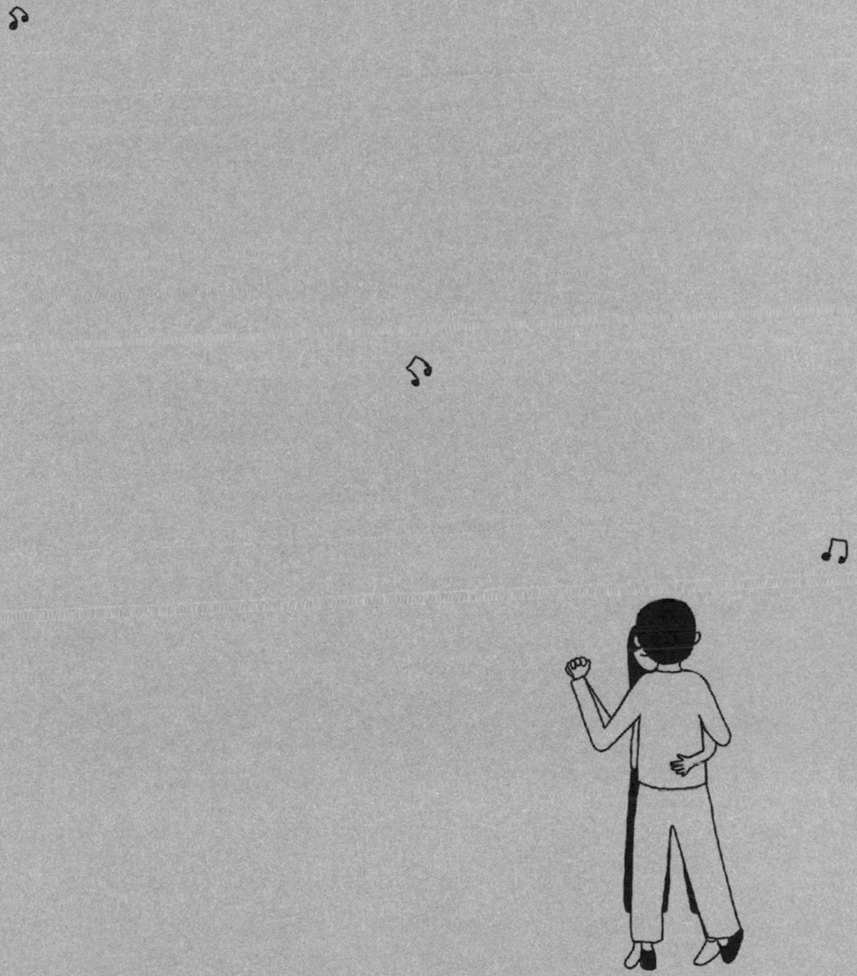

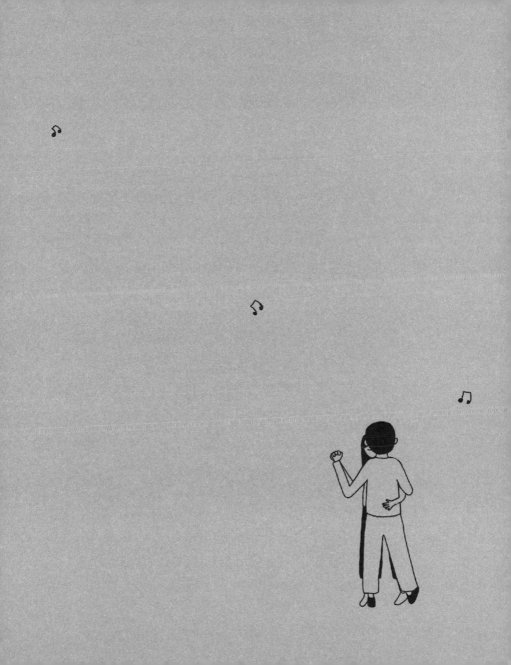

FIND SOMETHING
OR SOMEONE THAT
MAKES YOU LAUGH.

EVEN (ESPECIALLY)
WHEN YOU'D
SOONER CRY.

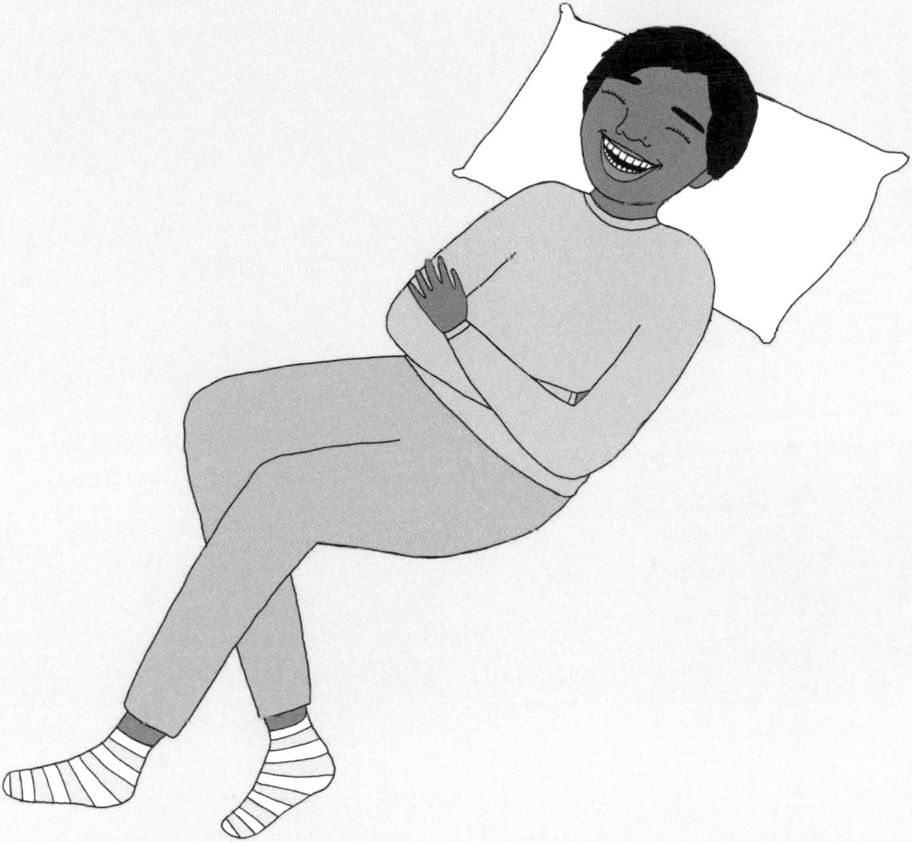

TAKE A RISK.

SEND THE TEXT.

DON'T EVER
FEEL GUILTY
FOR PUTTING
YOURSELF FIRST.

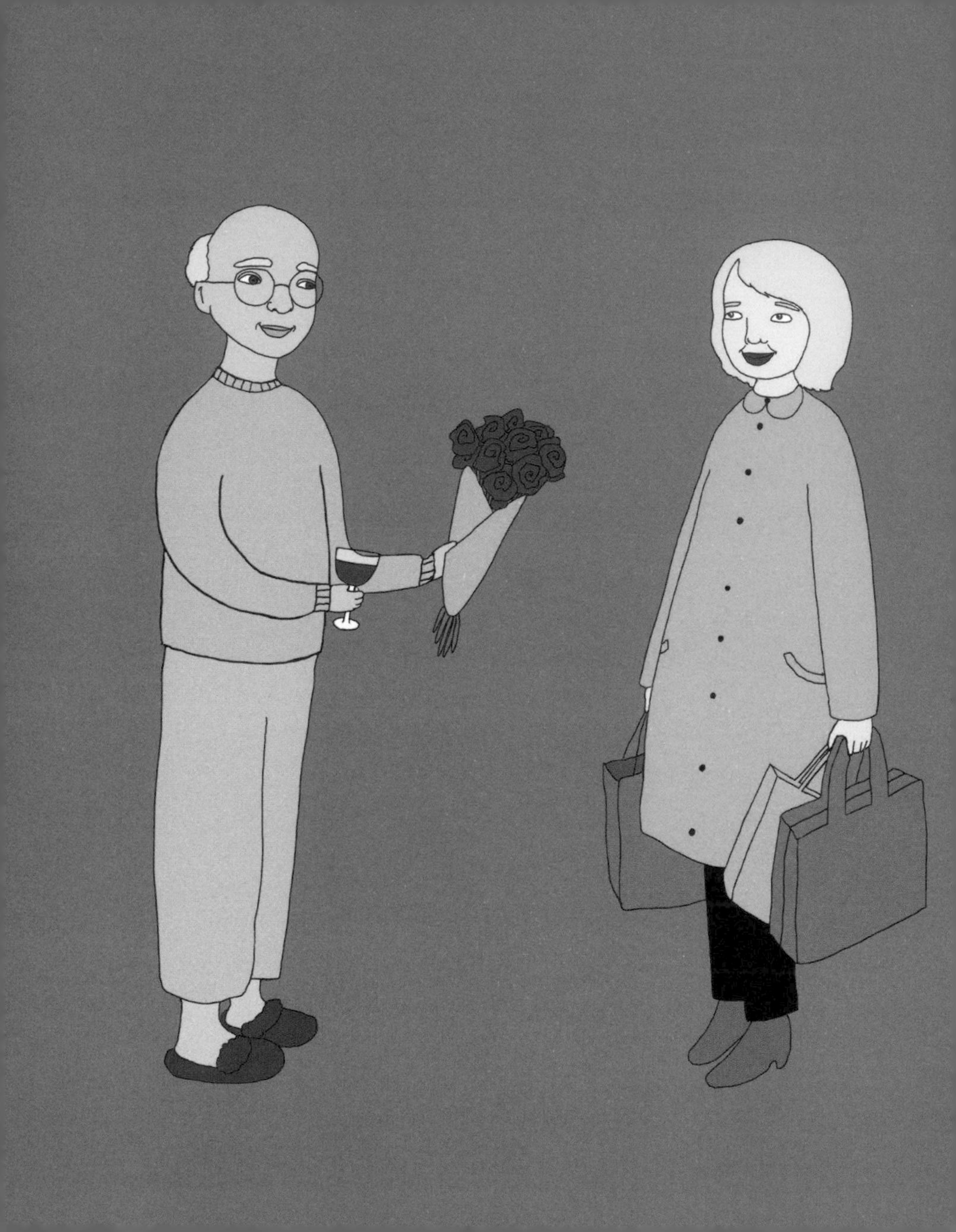

EVEN ON THE
LONGEST OF DAYS,
MAKE SURE THERE
IS ENOUGH LOVE LEFT
FOR THOSE CLOSEST
TO YOU.

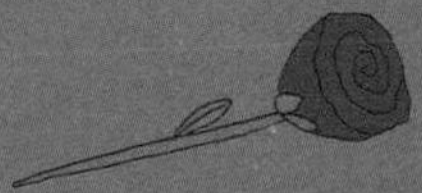

YOUR FAMILY IS
WHOEVER
YOU LOVE.

HELP

EACH OTHER.

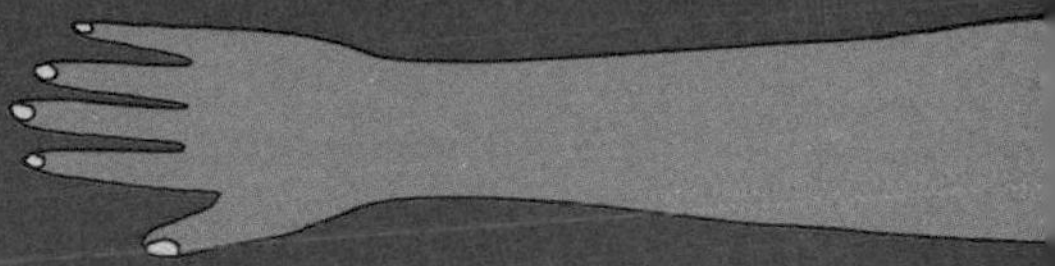

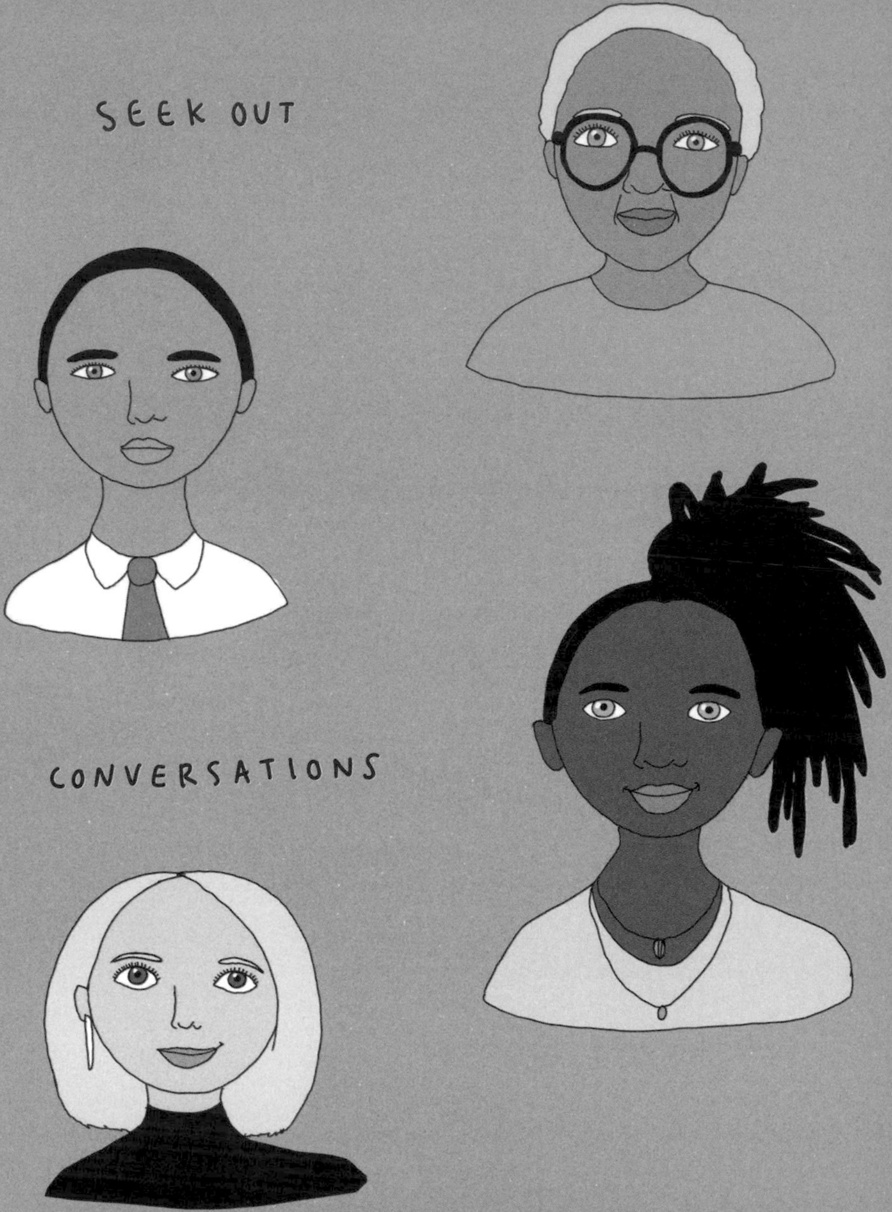
SEEK OUT
CONVERSATIONS

WITH PEOPLE

WHO DON'T

LOOK LIKE YOU.

THIS IS YOUR SPACE.
BLOCK WHOEVER YOU NEED TO.
ONLY FOLLOW WHAT
INSPIRES YOU AND MAKES
YOUR HEART SING.

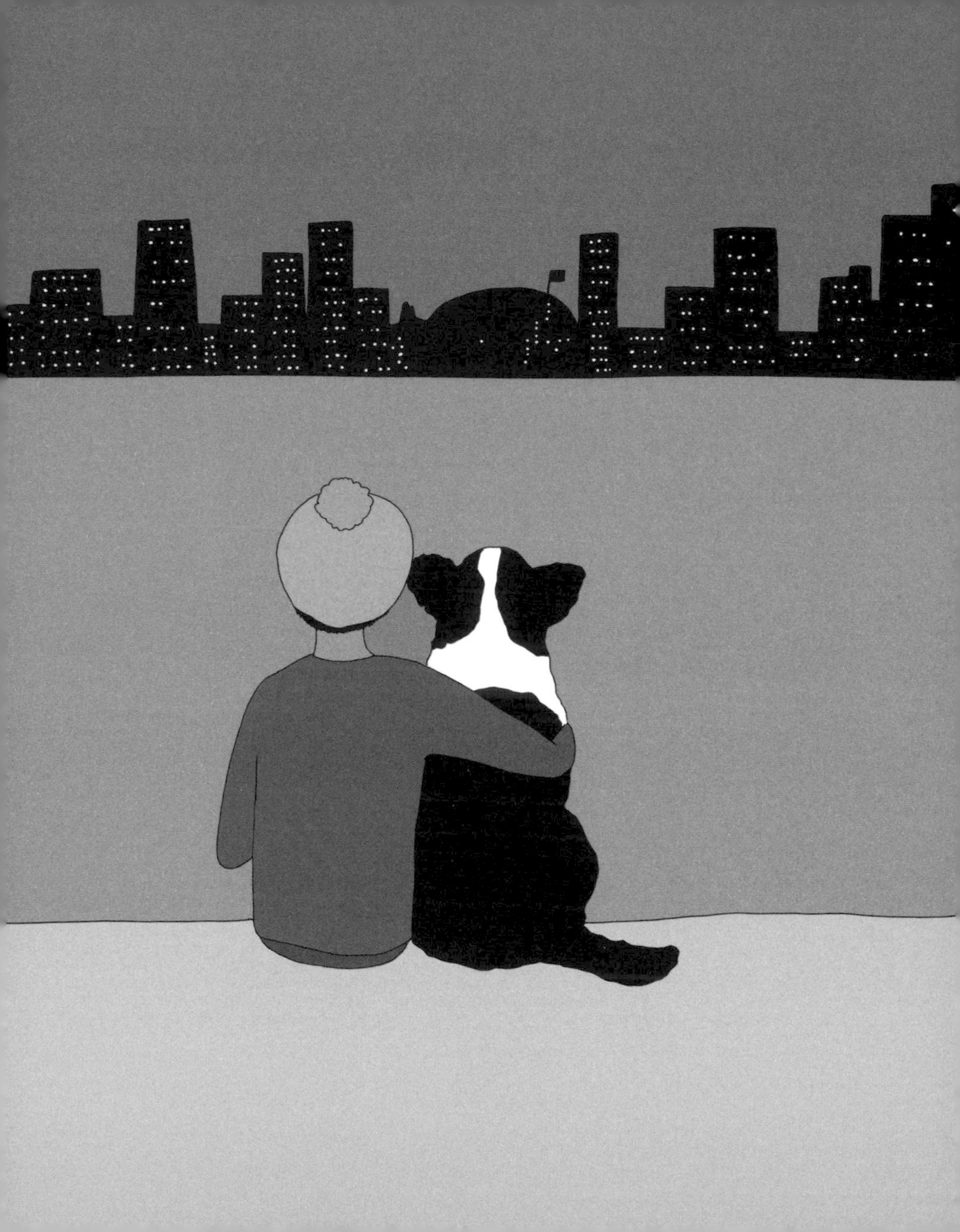

FIND SOMEONE
WHO WILL
LISTEN.

NEVER UNDERESTIMATE
THE POWER OF GETTING
LOST IN SOMEONE ELSE'S
WORDS.

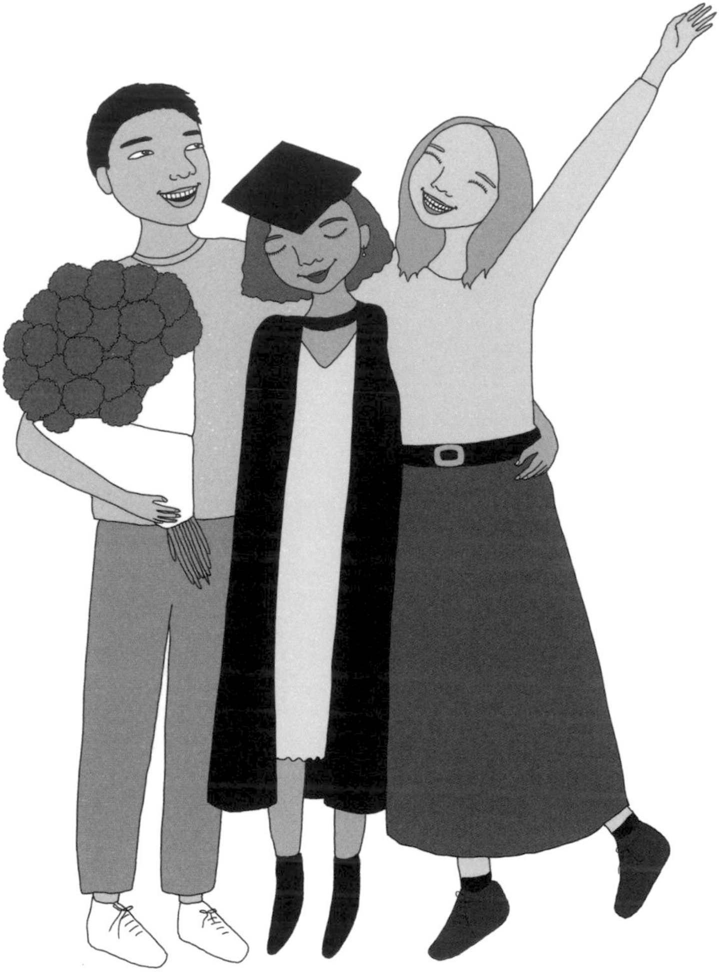

SURROUND YOURSELF
WITH PEOPLE WHO ARE
NOT THREATENED BY
YOUR SUCCESS BUT
INSTEAD LIFT YOU UP
AND CELEBRATE RIGHT
BY YOUR SIDE.

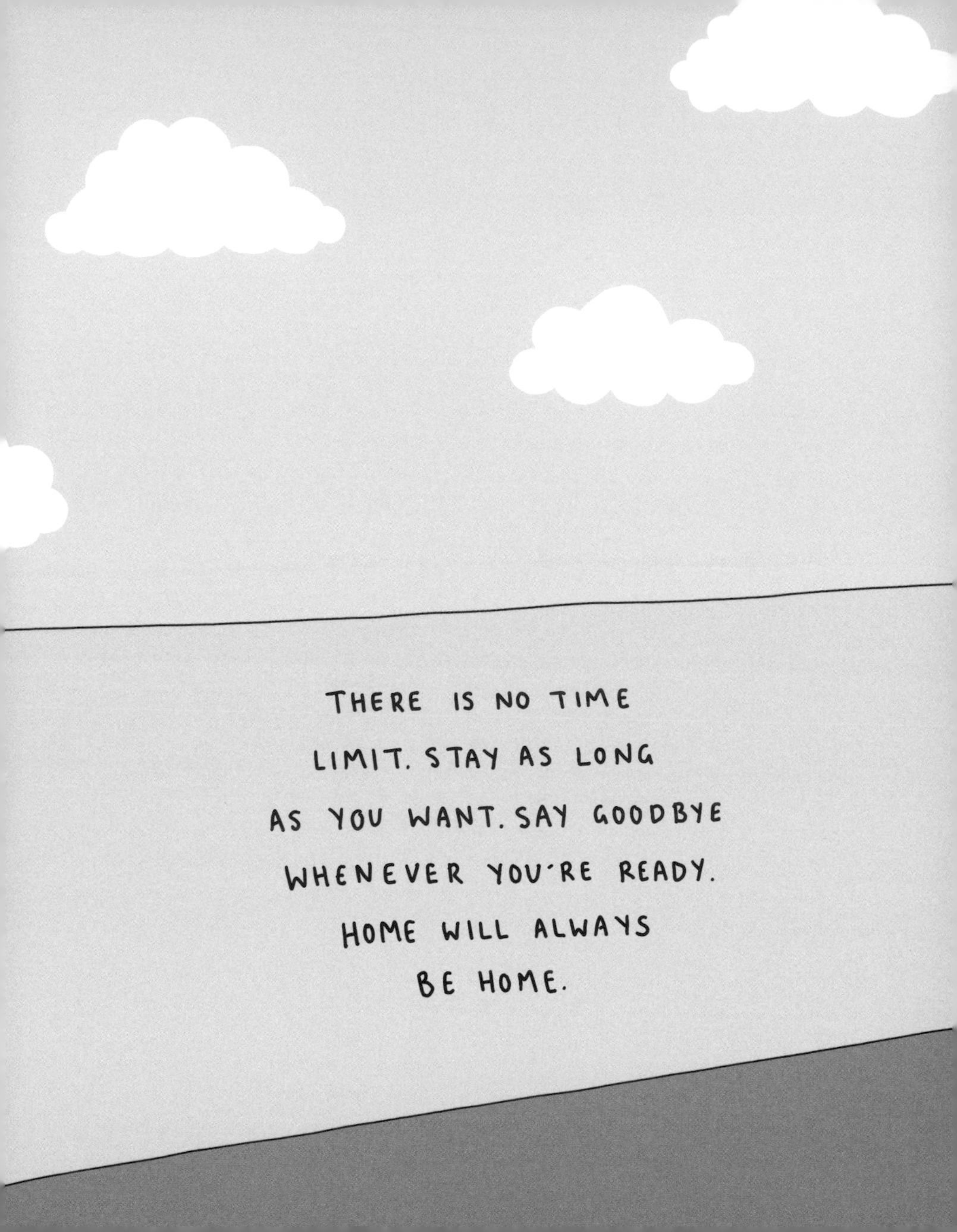
THERE IS NO TIME
LIMIT. STAY AS LONG
AS YOU WANT. SAY GOODBYE
WHENEVER YOU'RE READY.
HOME WILL ALWAYS
BE HOME.

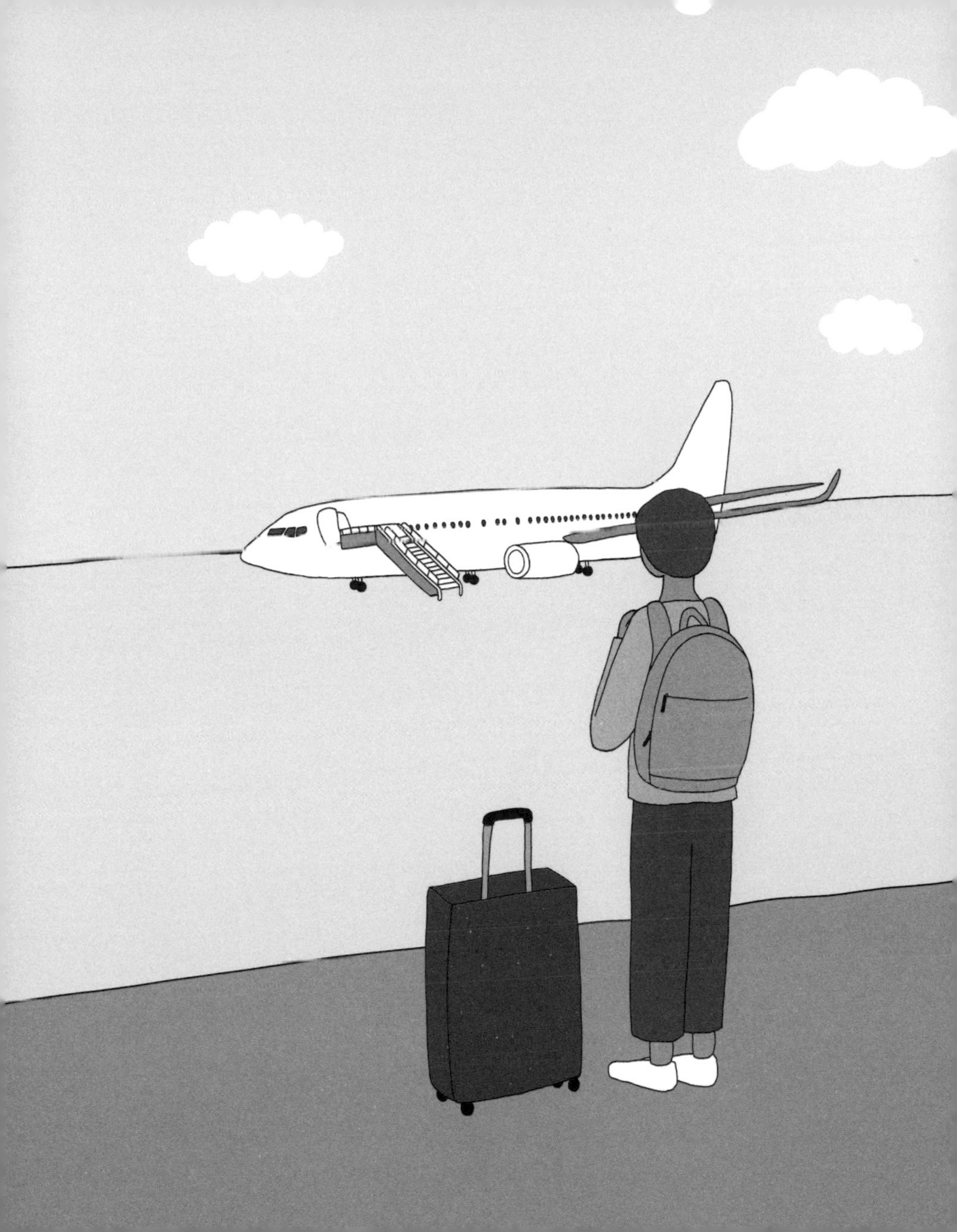

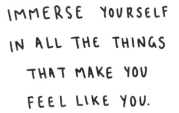

IMMERSE YOURSELF
IN ALL THE THINGS
THAT MAKE YOU
FEEL LIKE YOU.

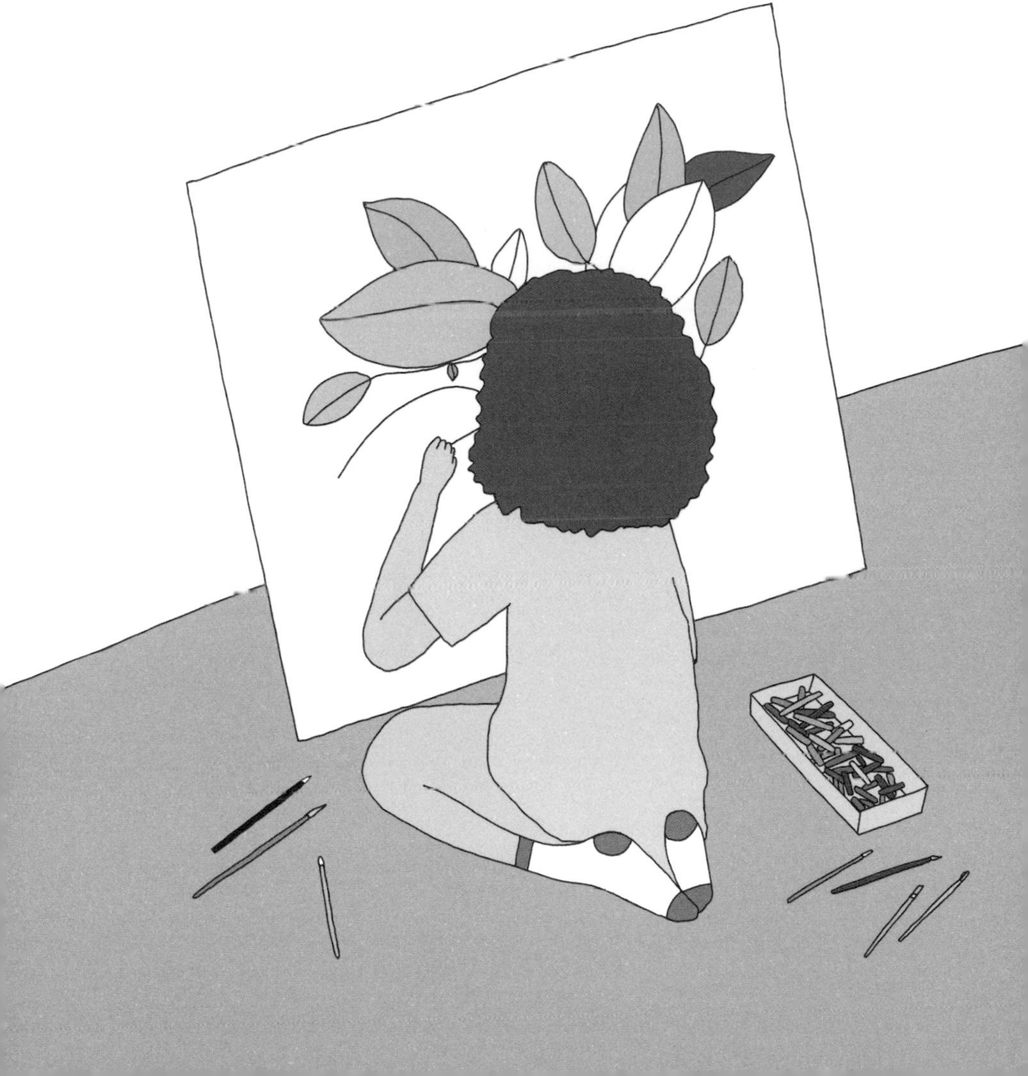

YOU'RE BRAVER
THAN YOU THINK
YOU ARE.

DON'T WORRY ABOUT
TWO OR FIVE OR TEN
YEARS FROM NOW.
JUST ENJOY BEING
IN THIS MOMENT,
RIGHT HERE, RIGHT NOW.

TAKE OFF YOUR SHOES.
MAKE A CUP OF TEA.
TURN OFF YOUR PHONE.
PUT ON SOME MUSIC.
LOOK OUT THE WINDOW.
LOOK AT THE CLOUDS.
LOOK AT THE GRASS.
LOOK AT THE MOON.
LOOK AT THE TREES.
FORGET ALL THE NOISE.
FORGET THE BAD NEWS.
IT'S OKAY TO STILL ENJOY
GOOD THINGS, EVEN WHEN
IT FEELS LIKE THE WHOLE
WORLD IS FALLING APART.

POUR AS MUCH
LOVE AS YOU CAN
INTO THE WORLD
EVERY SINGLE DAY.

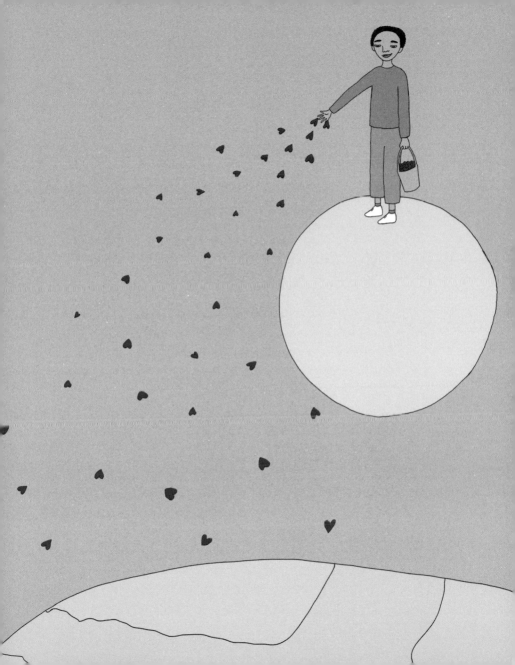

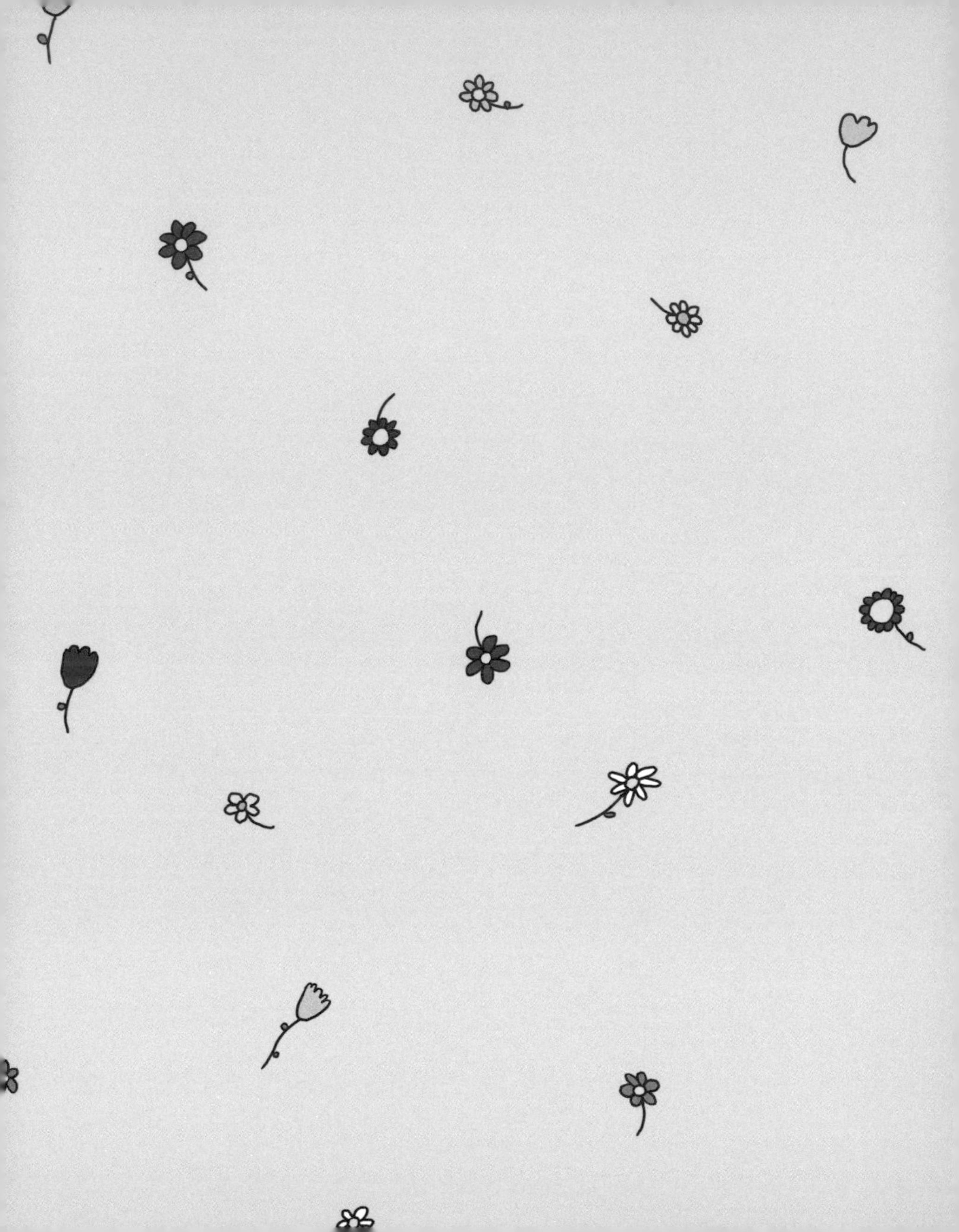

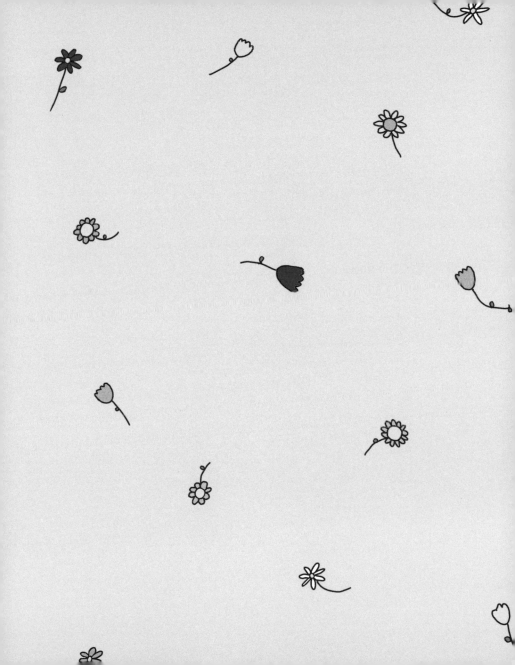

WE'RE RIGHT HERE
WITH YOU.

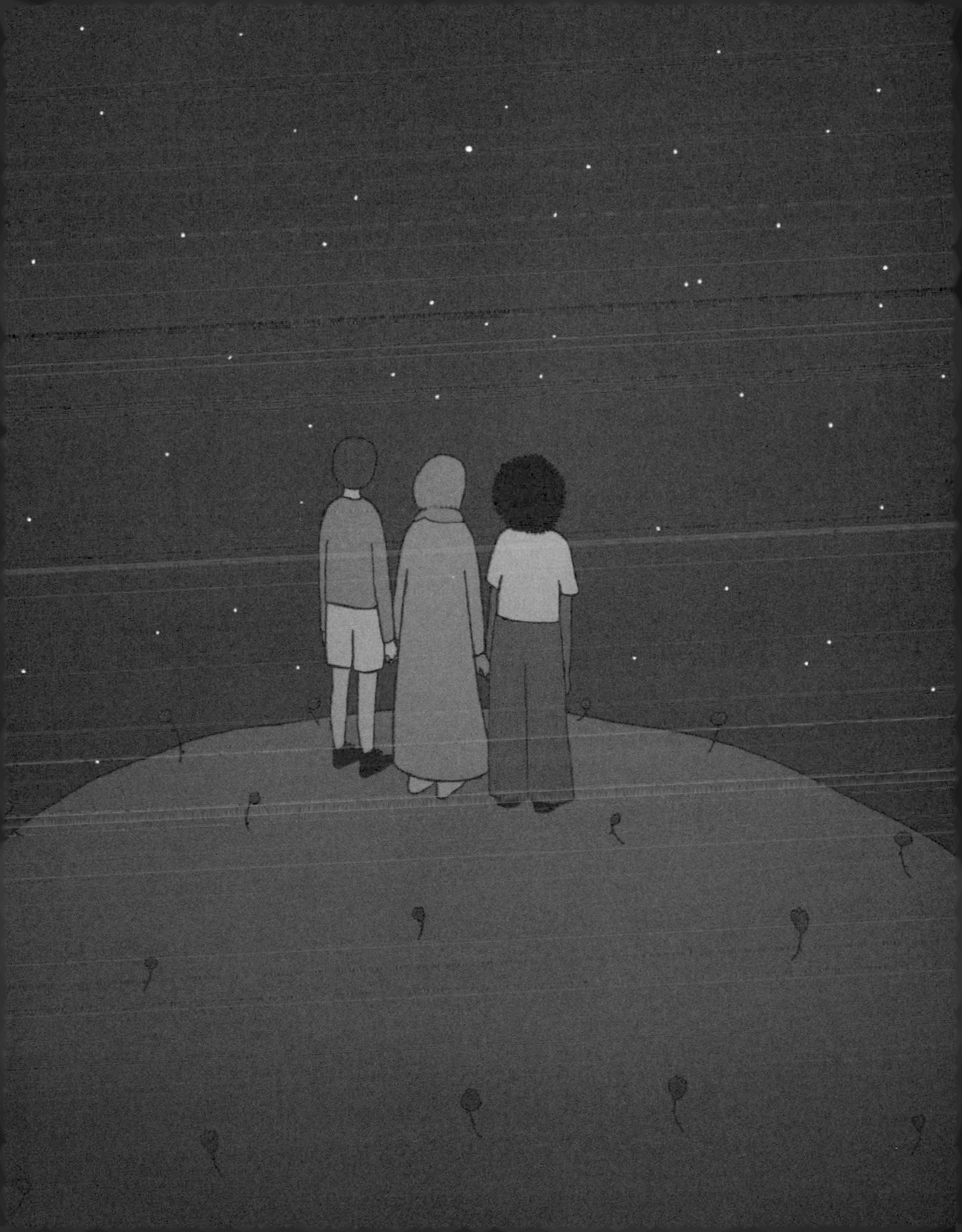

ACKNOWLEDGEMENTS

Thank you to my mum and dad who have shown me every single day of my life what it means to be kind, compassionate, generous and accepting of anyone and everyone. Thank you to my big brother who has protected me and inspired me from day one. Thank you to my grandparents for passing on your love of art and words to all of us. Thank you to each and every member of my beautiful, enormous family, I love you all. Thank you to my friends for reminding me to laugh and reminding me to dance. Thank you to all of my teachers, especially Jenny Webb for being my Miss Honey. To Claire Murdoch, Rachel Eadie, Grace Thomas, Cat Taylor and the whole team at Penguin Random House, thank you for believing in me and seeing magic in this book. Thank you to Anna Montague, Judith Curr, Gideon Weil, Laina Adler, Suzanne Quist, Yvonne Chan and everyone at HarperOne for taking this book on a whole new journey across the world. Thank you to the team at Isentia. Thank you to everyone around the world who has sent me a kind message or said anything positive. Thank you to anyone reading this who has ever thought about giving up but hasn't. I am so proud of you, keep going. ♥

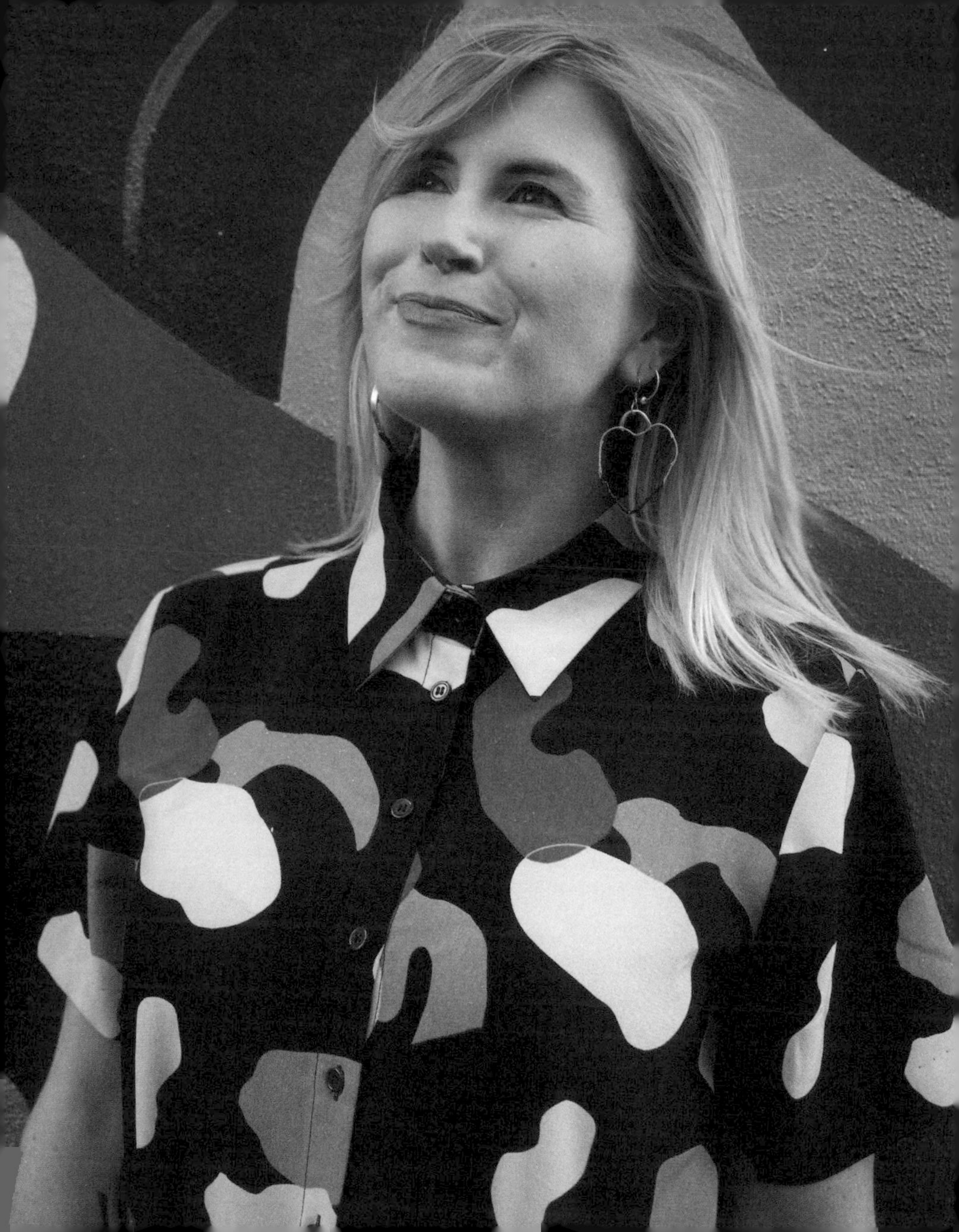

RUBY JONES

Ruby Jones is a young Wellington-based artist and writer whose messages of hope and kindness captured the zeitgeist and gained worldwide attention after the March 2019 Christchurch terrorist attacks, when she shared her illustration featuring two women embracing, penned with the words "This is your home and you should have been safe here." A few days on from the attacks, Ruby was asked to illustrate a cover for *Time* magazine. Since then, her work has been shared widely and has appeared online with BuzzFeed, i-D, *Vogue*, *Marie Claire* and *Nadia* magazine. This is her first book.

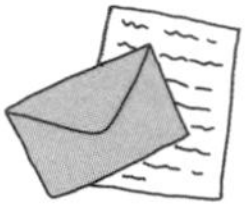

HarperCollins books may be purchased for educational, business, or sales promotional use. For information, please email the Special Markets Department at SPsales@harpercollins.com.

Originally published by Penguin Random House New Zealand, 2019

First US edition published in 2021

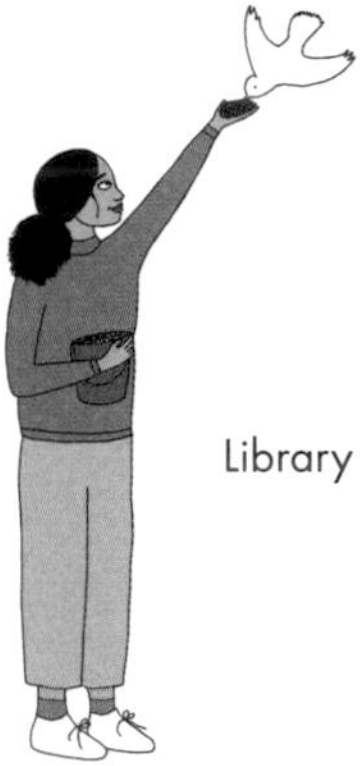

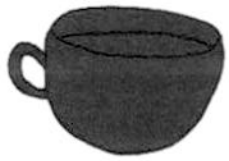

Text and cover design by Cat Taylor and Ruby Jones

Author photograph by Ruby Rowe

Library of Congress Cataloging-in-Publication Data has been applied for.

ISBN 978-0-06-304249-0

21 22 23 24 25 WOR 10 9 8 7 6 5 4 3 2 1